# WOMEN OF SUBSTANCE

## PROFILES OF ASIAN WOMEN IN THE UK

Pushpinder Chowdhry

HANSIB/ AWP

Published in 1997 jointly by Hansib Publications
Tower House, 141-149 Fonthill Road, London N4 3HF
and Asian Women in Publishing (AWP)
56 Paines Lane, Pinner, Middx HA5 3BT

Printed in the United Kingdom by The Bracken Press, Hatfield.
Production by Cut & Paste DTP Services, Welwyn.
Cover design by Stefan Brazzo Design and Print, Cheshunt.

© Pushpinder Chowdhry, 1997

British Library Cataloguing in Publication Data.
A catalogue record for this book is available from the British Library.

ISBN 1-870518-56-X

# Dedication

*This book is dedicated to my mother, Harinder Kaur,
whose love, courage and determination has been
the source of inspiration for this book.*

# Reason for Publishing

To mark the 50th anniversary of India and Pakistan's
Independence on 15th August, 1947.

# Acknowledgements

MANY THANKS to all the women who have participated in this book, without whom this book would not have been possible.

Special thanks to whizz kid Sara Bains for her patience, understanding and for sensitivity with regards to the subject matter.

I would also like to thank Dhanwant Ranchi, Roshan Horabin, Annalies Kramer, Sharmila Kohli and Bilay Want for their help in times of crisis.

Special thanks to my children Virahn, Heteash and Vaani who provided the enthusiasm and willingly accepted the constraints on my time.

To my husband, Chanchal, who continued to advise and motivate me and expects no thanks!

And finally to Arif Ali of Hansib Publications for providing the opportunity to jointly publish **WOMEN OF SUBSTANCE**.

# WOMEN OF SUBSTANCE

## PROFILES OF ASIAN WOMEN IN THE UK

**Background**

**Introduction**

**Foreword**

*(by Rt. Hon Harriet Harman MP, Minister for Women)*

**"Women of Substance"**

*Alphabetically pages 10 to 155*

**Brief profiles**

*Pages 156 to 158*

**Names and addresses**

# Background

THIS BOOK is a serious attempt to chronicle the achievements of some of the Asian women in Britain. Profiling over 200 women, it is hoped that our next edition will have many more. For the purpose of this book, Asian refers to South Asian women who originally came from the Indian Subcontinent - India, Pakistan, Sri Lanka and Bangladesh. It also includes women who had migrated to East Africa before coming to settle in Britain. It covers a vast geographical and heterogeneous group of women comprising of diverse cultural backgrounds, religions, languages, castes and sects, which contributes to their individual life experiences.

For many women in Britain, their cultural identities are paradoxically challenged by new experiences and boundaries, providing a sense of common identity and unity.

The methods used to collect data were random and selection was subjective. Women were approached through community networks and organisations. Further research was carried out through back dated issues of Asian newspapers and magazines collected at libraries and other resource centres. Advertisements and articles were placed in Asian media, inviting women to participate or nominate suitable candidates for the profiles.

Through the experience of being an immigrant having faced struggle and isolation, some chose to work within the community to help others, as COMMUNITY WORKERS, they worked in day centres, Asian women's refuges, counselling schemes and with campaigning groups.

EDUCATION seems to be a popular option. As headteachers and teachers working alongside authorities and parents, mediating with children, representing them and voicing their needs. Providing sensor points for training, promoting and advise to other professionals.

In MEDICINE, they provide an anchor in confrontational concerns relating to religious and cultural practices. As consultant doctors, physicians and health workers, they are feeding their knowledge back into the profession, contributing to the general health of the nation.

Many have opted for the field of LAW and have channelled their skills to campaign against institutional racism and sexism within the judicial system.

Through LITERATURE, female writers are using the power of the written word to express their feelings, promoting incontestable and powerful images to dispel the negativity within their community and in the indigenous population.

In ARTS, women are using their life experiences through painting, sculpture, music, dance and film. They are providing a positive and accessible means to communicate and use the Arts to develop an understanding of living in a multicultural Britain.

In POLITICS, as elected councillors they are making legislative changes possible, that affect the ethnic minorities. Some have reached the high office of Mayor, whilst there is representation of a Life Peer in the House of Lords.

Empowered with self confidence and hard work, they have been able to enter the male dominated BUSINESS world. In doing so, they own and operate their own business, fulfilling personal goals and ambitions, whilst making a contribution to the British economy. The creation of wealth has also meant facilitating a 'trickle down' effect through Charity and fundraising events both in Britain and abroad.

Above all, they have been successful at all levels including SPORT and intertwining western ways into the Asian value system in their daily life.

# Introduction

A SIGNIFICANT number of Asian women are now becoming visible in Politics, Business, Arts and Media in the City as well as Science and Academia. The backgrounds of the women profiled in this book are diverse, each with her own social, cultural and religious upbringing which forms a part of their individual experiences.

This celebration of finding so many Asian women in a position of being positive role models for the young and their peer groups, generates a powerful message.

Profiles of these very special women range from shop floor trade union activists to successful business women, consultants, painters, writers and housewives keeping family relationships going through difficult circumstances. All these women have been driven by the need to prove themselves and are managing to push the boundaries, shattering many a stereotype by penetrating through the "glass ceiling" of inequality.

These success stories have been a long time coming, although it has been a hard and difficult struggle as Asian women had to try much harder than their contemporaries to be accepted. For many, the personal struggle to success has generated internal conflict and stress. A tendency towards self doubt and continuous attacks of guilt when leaving young children to go to work, almost always made them question whether sacrifices were proving to be too much.

Some women give up their careers temporarily to start a family, returning only after skilfully negotiating child care. These women have proved that it is possible to successfully do both, whilst others survived divorce and managed a career or a business, providing emotional and financial security for their families. Many pursued their careers and alternative lifestyles, rejecting marriage, to suit their individual needs.

As well as gaining success for their own personal achievements, these women are seen to be sharing and feeding their success back into the community. In doing so they provide positive images, while they augment and consolidate their Asian identity, rather than compromise it. Showing pride in their cultural heritage, they have proved that there is no reason to forego ones religious or cultural practices in order to attain their goals.

As "Women of Substance" they have shown courage and sheer determination to have made their achievements possible, changing the way Asian women are perceived. These are the women who have led the way, but despite these successes Asian women still have a long way to go!

**Pushpinder Chowdhry**
London, July 1997

# Foreword

BRITAIN has not made it easy for women to achieve. Nor have their achievements generally been publicly recognised. The obstacles they have had to overcome, and the hard choices they have had to make along the road to success, have all too frequently been overlooked.

In refreshing contrast, this collection of profiles paints a fascinating picture of the special contributions Asian women have made and continue to make to life in Britain today. They have made a difference in all corners of life, sometimes very visibly in high profile public positions, sometimes less so in their support for people in need or in their fight against injustice.

Women of substance is a source of celebration and inspiration. Celebration of the wealth of achievement that shines from these pages; inspiration in showing us all, young and old, Asian and non-Asian, just what can be possible. These women have pushed back the boundaries for their own generation as well as for those to come.

I hope this book will lead to new alliances, more networks, an increased recognition of Asian women's achievements in Britain and beyond, and - it should go without saying - to many new friendships. All this will enrich the dialogue which, as Minister for Women, I am keen to promote and participate in.

**Rt. Hon Harriet Harman MP**
Minister for Women

# WOMEN OF SUBSTANCE

## PROFILES OF ASIAN WOMEN IN THE UK

# Sudarshan Abrol

Sudarshan Abrol

Sudarshan Abrol was born in Punjab, India in 1937.

She graduated from Punjab University with a B Ed degree and a MA in Hindi. After teaching for just one year she was promoted to the position of Assistant District Inspector.

In 1963 Sudarshan came to settle in Britain and secured her first job at a Junior and Infant School, where she developed a particular interest in Special Education. This resulted in her studying for a certificate in Special Education. In 1968 she began teaching pupils with moderate Learning Difficulties but, after when failing to gain a promotion, went back to Primary Education as the Head of an English department.

The turning point came when after two years the school closed down, pushing Sudarshan to study for a M.Ed (Master of Special Education) at Birmingham University, which led to the opportunity to Head a Middle School for children with moderate learning difficulties in Walsall. Later she become Deputy Head as a Special School in Solihull. During her seven year stay, Sudarshan was unsuccessful in nine applications for Headship, but her perseverance was rewarded when in 1983 she was appointed Head Teacher at Mayfield School - a special needs school, catering for pupils with severe learning disabilities, most of whom are from the ethnic minorities.

Sudarshan's commitment to Special Education can be seen in her determination to provide the Mayfield Centre with on premises hydro, physio and speech therapy, something took seven years of persuasion and negotiation. In 1988, Sudarahan was awarded the MBE for Community Service.

Sudarshan now wants to pursue her interest in writing for Special Education and to work as an advocate on behalf of adults with learning disabilities.

# Sushma Dilip Acquilla

Sushma Dilip Acquilla

The daughter of a government officer, Sushma Dilip Acquilla, was born in Gwalior, India, in 1948. The family moved to Bhopal in the late 50s, where Sushma completed her secondary and medical education. She met her husband, Dilip Acquilla, while still a student and they married in 1972 a few days before her husband came to England.

Arriving in England the following year, Sushma worked in the hospital paediatrics until 1976. She faced difficulty in getting a senior post, as the consultant she worked for had firm ideas that a woman with children is best placed at home. Having three children in the mid-seventies she continued to work, feeling that any time taken out from a career in medicine, a fast moving science, would only jeopardise opportunities for the future. She was lucky to have the full support of her husband as well as good nannies.

In 1982 Sushma became a (Public Health) Registrar and progressed to Consultant in Community Medicine and lecturer in Epidemiology and Public Health in 1986. She was appointed a Director of Public Health in 1988, the first Asian woman to hold the position. In 1993, she was appointed as the consultant for post-graduate and continuing education in public Health medicine for the Northern region.

Sushma was invited to be a member of International Medical Commission on Bhopal (IMCB), a team of 14 experts in different fields from 11 countries. IMCB members visited Bhopal and conducted studies on the long term health effects among survivors of the city's gas disaster. The report was published in the National Medical Journal of India (NMJI) and the British Medical Journal (BMJ). Once published in NMJI, it was used as legal evidence. Sushma and another colleague were invited to present the case in the Indian Supreme Court on behalf of the victims. They won their case and the recommendations of IMCB are to help determine future health care provision for the victims.

Sushma's work has also been presented to the international scientific community and won the Baum prize for outstanding work in environmental epidemiology in Germany, having been invited as a keynote speaker in the European Environmental Epidemiology Symposium in 1996.

Alongside her work in Epidemiology and Public Health, Sushma is a trustee to the Aycliffe School (a special needs school) and an independent governor to the Local Teesside Tertiary College.

She also supports her husband, who set up a Society of Indian Doctors in Cleveland, which is active in raising funds for charities in both the UK and India.

# Bushra Ahmed

"Nothing has been handed to me on a plate - I had to prove my worth" are words which sum up Bushra Ahmed, Marketing Director at The Legendary Joe Bloggs Inc. Co. and music artist manager.

Born in Karachi, Pakistan in 1961 her family moved to England in 1963 when her father, an RAF Engineer, was posted to Lancashire. Within a year of arriving the family had started trading in the fashion business. At the age of eight, when most girls were playing with their dolls, Bushra was a Sales Assistant, by 15 she was managing and buying for the family's Burnley shop.

In 1977, the family moved to Manchester where they

opened their cash & carry business "Pennywise" which is still trading today. Bushra left school at the same time because the business was expanding and has no regrets. Unity and loyalty to ones family were her parents dictum and their children were inspired and thrived on it.

It wasn't long before Bushra learned all aspects of the fashion business and was running the whole shop and in 1986 Bushra found her "true niche in life" when Joe Bloggs Inc. Co was created. As Marketing Director, Bushra employed a team of publicists to work with her to launch the brand and to maintain its' credibility.

Fashion, music and a little more than a hint of business acumen are a powerful combination and Bushra's knowledge of all three charged the success of the company. Sponsoring talented up-and-coming bands it was only natural that when they achieved success Joe Bloggs did too. It is now an established label in Britain and is also sold throughout Europe, Asia and Australia with it's next stop being America.

Music being as great a passion as Joe Bloggs, Bushra has managed a female Asian solo artist, Sabina for the last ten years.

When time allows, Bushra enjoys go-karting, eating fine cuisine, travelling and of course shopping.

Stating "absolutely everything I am today is because of my parents", it is not incorrect to assume that they have been her inspiration; her father who treated all his children as equals and with respect and her mother her perfect role model.

# Samira Ahmed

Samira Ahmed was born in 1968 and brought up in London. Educated at Wimbledon High School for Girls, she went on to St Edmund Hall, Oxford where she read English. Continuing her studies, she completed her postgraduate diploma in newspaper journalism at City University, after which she joined the BBC as a news trainee in 1990.

After working as a presenter for World Service Television News and a reporter for Newsnight, Samira became a news correspondent in 1994, covering general news for network radio and television.

Her spare time is spent reading and catching the latest movies at the cinema.

# Veeda Ahmed

Veeda Ahmed, a fine artist, who we interviewed in her studio in Battersea, London, has remained totally engrossed and committed to painting for the last twenty years. Her love of Fine

Art began in school in the 1960s whilst studying at the Convent of Jesus and Mary in Lahore, Pakistan, where she won the first of many fine art prizes.

Veeda then went on to gain two first class degrees at the University of the Punjab, Lahore, Pakistan. In the Bachelor of Fine Art degree (1972) she was given a scholarship by the university and went on to be awarded the gold medal for her Master of Fine Arts (1974).

In 1974 she came to study at the Ruskin School of Drawing and Fine Art at Oxford University. Veeda has resided in England since 1990 where she has regularly exhibited with the Chelsea Art Society.

She has to date participated in 18 group shows all over Pakistan and England. Her first solo exhibition was held at the Barbican in London. Her paintings are in private collections in Pakistan, England, Kuwait, Philippines and the USA.

Her most recent exhibition was a group show at the Silverthorne Studios.

# Anjana Ahuja

Anjana Ahuja was born in London in 1969 and brought up in Harlow, Essex, where she was educated at the town's state schools. Gaining 5 'A' levels at Harlow College, she went on to Imperial College, London University to study physics, gaining a PhD in space physics.

During this period she began freelancing as a science writer, winning several writing prizes. On receiving her doctorate in 1993, she switched careers, attending a newspaper journalism course at City University, London, sponsored by the Guardian.

Anjana spent a short time on the Crewe Chronicle, a weekly newspaper in Cheshire, before being offered jobs as a trainee reporter at the BBC and The Times. She chose to join The Times in August 1994 and in May 1995 was made a staff feature writer specialising in science, technology and medicine. She has a weekly technology column and also writes news stories, book reviews and travel pieces and occasionally appears on radio.

She enjoys walking, aerobics, cooking and entertaining.

# Raj Kumari Ahuja

Daughter of a wealthy businessman who was named Darbari Shah (King of Business), Raj Kumari Ahuja was born in Lyallpur in 1938. At the time of partition, her family had to flee, eventually settling down in Indore in 1947.

As a young girl, despite their hardship, Raj Kumari helped her mother with social and community work, visiting orphanages and temples.

Educated by her elder brother and motivated and supported by her mother, she completed her medical degree from MGM College, Indore in 1962. Following her marriage in 1964, she arrived in Britain, settling in Wigan, Greater Manchester. Encouraged by her husband to study further, Raj Kumari completed a course in family planning in 1967.

Raj Kumari Ahuja

Joining her husband as a principal GP at his practice in 1970, she focused on the wellbeing of her patients, which has always been of the utmost importance. In 1972, she became a medical officer in family planning and was involved in teaching medical students.Wanting to diversify into other areas of medicine, she studied for a diploma in Tropical Medicine and Hygiene at Liverpool University in 1973. Appointed Clinical Assistant in obstetrics and gynaecology the same year, she continued in this role until 1988. She gave up her teaching post in 1993.

In 1989, Raj Kumari won the British Medical Association Photographic Clinical Congress Award to attend the BMA conference in Jamaica. Two years later, she was awarded 'Hind Rattan' for outstanding services, contribution and achievements. In 1995 won the Gastrocare Lederle award to attend the American Gastroenterology Association Congress, held in San Diego, USA.

Since embarking on her medical career, Raj Kumari has been extensively involved in developing her own fundholding practice, where she is lead GP, and auditing other practices. As Chairperson from 1987 to 1994 and currently President of the Wigan Division of Overseas Doctors Association, she was awarded Fellowship of the ODA in 1994 and also remains an executive committee member of the National ODA. She is Vice Chairperson of the Women Doctors' Forum through which she promotes gender and racial equality and has attended national and international BMA and ODA conferences.

Raj Kumari uses her expertise to educate Asian viewers in Hindi, through a television presentation on family planning, and throughout her time in Britain she has been actively involved in religious and community work. She continues to maintain contact with India, involving herself in social and community work there and in Britain, especially with women's charities.

Raj Kumari's personal reward in life, because of her interest in human rights, is that her daughter now works with Amnesty International, thus fulfilling Raj's dreams.

# Najma Akhtar

Najma Akhtar, winner of the 1984 Asian song contest and recipient of a Gold disc for outstanding sales in the UK, was born in Chelmsford, a quiet English village in the Essex countryside. At first a bit of a culture shock for her parents, who moved there from the hustle and bustle of London, it is now very much home for all the family.

After studying for a Master of Chemical Engineering degree at Aston University in Birmingham and an MSc at Southbank University, Najma focused on her love for music, thus beginning a career in singing that has transcended languages and styles.

Multi-lingual, she sings ghazal and jazz arrangements and semi-classical styles in Urdu, Punjabi, Gujrati and English and has recorded with many well known artists.

Since her big career break in 1984, Najma has successfully released five albums world-wide and travels extensively to give personal performances, with her biggest market being Japan.

While most of Najma's spare time is spent developing her art: composing songs and listening to music, she is able to serve as a role model to the younger generation by lecturing on music and organising music workshops.

## Amar

Teenage singing sensation, Amar, who shot to fame at the age of 14 with her Hindi rendition of Whitney Houston's I Will Always Love You, was born and brought up in Birmingham.

Being the daughter of bhangra star, Mangal Singh, it should come as no surprise that her love of composing and singing comes from her father, who motivates and encourages her in all her endeavours.

The success of her Hindi rendition was picked up by the Warner label, Blanco y Negro, who have since signed an exclusive £3m deal with her. At 17, this contract puts Amar into the record books as one of the first Asian girls to be signed by a major label in this country.

With a voice that resembles that of Lata Mangeshkar, her first Warner single already out and a debut album planned for the Summer, she is a priority artist for the company.

## Anita Anand

Anita Anand, whose interest in politics and social issues began as a child, was born in London in 1972.

Remembering the political arguments around the dinner table, and at school, she involved herself in debates, which led her to writing freelance contributions to different publications and holding several posts as an editor.

Originally intending to study law, she graduated in English Literature at Kings College, University of London, and went on to win the Best Speaker in Great Britain Award for the English

Anita Anand

Speaking Union and National Westminster cup for public speaking. She also secured an ESU scholarship to study at Harvard University in America.

As fate would have it, her career took off in journalism immediately after leaving university, when Anita began freelancing for TV Asia, now Zee TV. Successfully securing the post of a full-time research assistant and later as a reporter, she has produced and presented high-profile interviews with the likes of Benazir Bhutto and Makhtar Ahmed (the east London race attack victim) since becoming head of news and current affairs for Zee TV.

One of the highlights of her career has been receiving the Guardian Award for her writing skills. A multi-lingual fluent in Hindi, English, French and German, she has access to a wide range of reading material.

Committed to the need to end the highlighting of differences between cultures as a means of dividing them within society, Anita accepts a many opportunities to speak at events held by social and community organisations as possible.

## Anupama Anand

Anupama Anand

Born in 1967 in the Indian capital of Delhi, Anupama Anand graduated from Miranda House, Delhi University in 1987. She arrived in Britain in 1990, settling in London. Appointed by Sunrise Radio, she wrote dramas, stories and voice make overs for many advertisements.

In 1991, she married and, in 1992, became the UK's first Asian television Hindi newscaster. In the same year, she became a mother to a beautiful daughter. In 1994, TV Asia changed hands and she became a presenter for the very popular Asian Morning programme, within which she interviewed a variety of people from film stars to local politicians. With this programme came media attention and she was asked to speak at and inaugurate prestigious ceremonies.

Wishing to diversify, Anupama took on a stage role and acted in a play based on India's well known Mantos stories, which received excellent reviews. The success of this play brought a change of direction in her career and she is currently writing a stage play and intends to act in more plays in the future.

## Indira Anand

Indira Anand, who strongly believes that, if we keep ourselves in tune with the Divine Source, nothing can go wrong with us and our whole life will be in harmony, was born in Lahore when it was part of India.

During her student days she actively participated in dramatics, debates and poetry, winning several inter-school, inter-college and inter-university prizes. She also represented the Delhi State in Volleyball at various tournaments and school and college at athletics.

She graduated with a BA (Hons) and MA in Economics from Delhi University and went on to the Hague, London, France, Denmark and Belgium on Government. of Netherlands and Rockfellers Foundation Fellowships for further studies towards a PhD and had to learn Dutch and Danish to carry out her research work.

Indira Anand

Indira married a textile technologist Subhash (currently professor of Textile and Director of Research) in 1967 and commenced her financial career in 1970 as an international economist and investment manager at CIS, progressing to head of international investment and foreign exchange in 1980. The time for a change came with her appointment as Assistant Director of Prudential Portfolio Management in 1985.

In 1987, Indira moved to Merrill Lynch Europe as Head of Japanese Sales and was promoted to Director of Equities, specialising in the Japanese market, for which she has studied conversational Japanese.

In her spare time, Indira teaches Yoga, which she trained for at Bihar School of Yoga and Hindi, on Saturday mornings to all age groups and different linguistic and racial background people.

Her love of poetry began in school days, writing on a variety of subject but, most recently, she has chosen the theme God and her relationship with God.

Not one to sit back, in her spare time Indira is currently learning to speak French, play the sitar and the art of spiritual healing.

# Nasim Anwar

Nasim Anwar, a Health Centre Manager, was born in Lahore, Pakistan in 1946.

Nasim came from a family of educationalists and, following family tradition, she went straight into higher education. She graduated from Pakistan Punjab University with a Bachelor of Arts.

Soon after marriage, Nasim and her husband emigrated to Britain. While her children were young she stayed at home as a full-time mother. It was during this period that she developed links with local schools while doing some voluntary work. This experience was to hold her in good stead when she got her first job as a classroom assistant. Her next post was as a Health Education Officer with Walsall Health Project where she acquired a Certificate in Health Education, Marital Counselling,

Bereavement Counselling and Care For The Elderly. As a Health & Social Welfare Officer at the UK Asian Woman's Conference, she attended courses in housing and immigration advice.

Nasim's next step was as a community advisor at the West Midlands Council for Disabled People. Following that she worked with UK Asian Women's Conference. as a Community Worker and then as a Co-ordinator. She has been an active member with the UKAWC for the last 13 years, holding responsible positions such as Secretary, Treasurer and Chairperson.

Presently she is a Centre Manager at Lansdowne Health Centre. Her responsibilities include managing the support service staff, the smooth running of the service equipment and the general profile of the Health Centre.

As an Asian woman in a managerial position, Nasim has encountered negativity among her fellow colleagues, but she has always dealt with this in a firm and calm manner, eventually earning respect through her excellent work. Nasim would like to progress within the management structure but always to a position with a certain amount of community links. She regularly attends refresher courses in leadership and team management.

Throughout her career, Nasim has always given priority to the education and welfare of her children and for this reason she often worked part-time. Her motto in life is "dedication and honesty".

# Leana Arain

Leana Arain was born in Kampala, Uganda where she underwent her early education.

As English education and qualifications were perceived the best, she was sent to the UK to study 'A' levels and continued until she graduated as BA(Hons) in Law at Southampton University. After completing her Barrister-at-Law at Middle Temple, Leana returned to Uganda in the 1960s.

Although the country seemed remote and austere, resolved to cope with its own problems and fulfill its aspirations in its own way, Leana found the beginning of independence for Uganda an exciting period of time. Leana's married, an active politician, who later became an MP and then Minister for the East African Community based in Tanzania.

Practising law with a British firm, Leana was to become the first female magistrate in Uganda in the late 1960s. Her husband was appointed High Commissioner for Uganda to the UK and it was at this time, sentimentally connected to Uganda and passionately involved with its children, that Leana set up the

Uganda Society for Disabled Children charity. Also as the Chairperson, she was involved in starting up Wives of African (OAV) Heads - AWAM, which raised £100,000 for African relief.

Leana and her husband were in Tanzania when the country was suddenly thrown into panic as Idi Amin came to power imposing dictatorship. The Asian community had become powerless and fearful for their lives. With Leana's husband's own life under threat and herself heavily pregnant, the couple escaped to Britain in the 1970s.

Dedicating time to raise her children and emotionally support her husband, Leana remained at home until the early 1980s when she undertook voluntary work around Windsor and Ascot, representing the Citizens Advice Bureau as a legal advisor on industrial law.

A move to London in the early 1990s prompted Leana to practise law again. Sadly, in 1994, her husband suffered a severe heart attack, resulting in Leana giving up full-time employment. Previously focusing her legal work on the British population at large, Leana has since decided she would specifically like to work with the ethnic communities.

# Gursowinder Ark

A pharmacist by profession, Gursowinder Ark, was born in Jallandar Punjab, India, where she spent her early years. When her parents left India for Britain, she stayed behind to finish her schooling at a prestigious boarding school in Dalhousie. Those years hold great memories of fun, freedom, midnight gatherings and learning Sanskrit 'parrot fashion'. Following school she did a one year correspondence course in interior designing.

Gursowinder Ark

Leaving India in early 70's to join her parents and brothers, she completed her school education and studied pharmacy at university. After graduation, Gus, as she is known, married and moved to Scotland where her husband works as G.P.

Her first professional post as a pharmacist was at a teaching hospital in Glasgow. After completion of an MSc., Gus specialised in Paediatrics and Infectious Diseases.

However, career minded as she was, she decided to give it all up in order to be a full-time mother to her two young children and has found this as rewarding as her hospital post.

In order to stay in touch with developments in pharmacy, Gus undertakes frequent locum work. She hopes to resume her full-time pharmacist career once her youngest son is at school and plans to branch off into community pharmacy so as to gain new experience.

# Anu Arora

Anu Arora

Born in Chandigarh in 1954, Anu is the youngest of two children. She and her elder sister both studied at a private English school in Chandigarh until the family moved to Britain in 1963.

Anu's interest in law stemmed from her father, who came to Britain to complete his law degree and undertake further studies for the Bar. Graduating from the University of Birmingham with an LLB (Hons) in 1977, she obtained her Bar Finals, Part II in London in 1978. Returning to the University of Birmingham, she undertook postgraduate studies and gained a PhD in 1982.

Much of her working life has been in the employment of the University of Liverpool, where she was initially offered a lecturing appointment in 1981. She then spent two years working at the University of London (Queen Mary College) before returning to the University of Liverpool in 1985. Having gained a number of promotions, Anu was awarded a personal chair by the University of Liverpool in 1996.

Anu Arora has published widely in the field of banking and commercial law. She has participated widely in seminars and lectures to lawyers and bankers and regularly acts as examiner within the University circuit and for the professional bodies.

Anu is married to a fellow academic in the Faculty of Medicine and has two young daughters.

# Rani Atma

Rani Atma

Rani Atma, director and founder of "The Asian Family Counselling Service" the only national marital service for the Asian community, was born in 1935 in Nairobi, Kenya.

Arriving in Britain in 1971, after completing her education in Nairobi, she decided to follow the career of counselling.

Rani trains other Asian women in counselling skills. She is a lay member of the General Medical Council, which allows her to sit on Professional Conduct Committee hearings. She is a firm believer in empowering women to assent their individuality

In her free time Rani enjoys reading, writing, gardening and swimming.

# Shamim Azad

Born in Bangladesh in 1951, Shamim Azad is a freelance writer, journalist and full-time teacher. having gained her BA Hons degree and MA from the University of Dhaka, Bangladesh, she arrived in Great Britain in1990 to teach in the London Borough of Tower Hamlets.

On Bangladesh Television she presented series of Children's programmes and also had a regular chat show. Her keen interest in writing has led to nine Publications of poetry, short stories, novels and collected essays in U.K. and Bangladesh.

In addition to teaching she is, currently working as an Overseas Correspondent in Daily Bhorer Kagoz, Bangladesh as a writer consultant for Half Moon (YPT) Young People's Theatre, her two bilingual plays toured around the U.K. and abroad. In 1995, she won fashion journalism award from 'Weekly Bichitra' Bangladesh's largest news weekly.

Married to Abul K. Azad a Chartered Accountant in 1972. She is a mother of two children - a girl Eeshita and a boy, Sajib.

Shamim loves watching musical shows and street performances. Radio addict. She also get engrossed with string-instrumental music. She enjoys book-reading in Valentine Park on long sunny days. She believes - 'in general women are more sensible creature than....'

Shamim Azad

# Ramola Bachchan

The foundations of her independent character having been formed very early in life, Ramola Bachchan is carrying on family tradition by running her own successful public relations management company in London.

Ramola was born in Calcutta, India in 1947 into a successful Sindhi business family and is the eldest of six children. Her father initially sent his children to the epitome of an English school in Calcutta, where they were exposed to a whole range of activities such riding, music lessons and ballet, before being sent to Loreto convent boarding school in Darjeeling.

At the age of eleven, Ramola went to a girls public school in England where she exhibited a flair for languages taking five at "O" level. As an all-rounder, Ramola participated in sports, debating and drama. At school she also helped to develop her cultural interest. During her "A" levels Ramola returned to India due to her father's failing health and there completed a degree in English Literature and Politics at Calcutta University.

Ramola Bachchan

Full time employment for the next five years was as a British Airways stewardess, which enabled her to gain new life experiences.

At 25 Ramola married Ajitabh Bachchan, a businessman from one of India's most notable families.

In 1987, Ramola and her family came to settle in Britain. Age never being an issue for a strong-minded person such as Ramola, she returned to college to do a Business Management degree at 38 and then at 40 she took up law, qualifying as a solicitor in London in 1994.

Variety being the spice of life, Ramola has also spent a few years as a TV and radio presenter for TV Asia in London hosting her own successful chat shows. Over the years she has organised countless, highly successful charity events in London, presenting celebrated Indian artists such as: Pandit Ravi Shankar, Ustad Zakir Hussain, Dr. L Subramaniam, Ustad Amjad Ali Khan to UK audiences.

At present Ramola is busy running her company RB Promotions. The aim of her company to "promote better links between India and the Western world" and she is excited by the enormous potential of this undertaking. However, Ramola feels bringing up her four children as "good human beings" is one of her most important achievements.

# Kamlesh Bahl

Kamlesh Bahl

Kamlesh Bahl, was born in Nairobi, Kenya in 1956 and is the current Chair Woman of the Equal Opportunities Commission.

Arriving in England at the age of nine, Kamlesh graduated in law from Birmingham University and went on to train as a solicitor with the Greater London Council.

She held a variety of posts in industry, including with the British Steel Corporation, Texaco Limited and Datalogic, while developing a parallel career in the public sector, starting as Chairman of the Law Society Commerce and Industry Group.

Kamlesh also served on the Law Society's Race Relations Committee and undertook a number of other public appointments.

Currently, a member of the No. 1 Diplomatic Service, Appeal Board of the Foreign and Commonwealth Office, Kamlesh is also a member of the Consultative Commission for Racism and Xenophobia established by the European court of ministers.

Her hobbies include music, dancing, swimming and travelling. She has been awarded CBE, for her work on equality issues.

# Rukhsana Bakhsh

Rukhsana Bakhsh

Rukhsana Bakhsh, an enthusiastic and committed teacher, was born in Peshawar, now Pakistan in 1944.Graduating in 1966 she went on to attain an MA in Psychology in 1968 followed by a BEd.

She arrived in Britain in 1970 as a young bride. After joining the Civil Service, Rukhsana started to feel settled and was soon promoted to Executive Officer and Section Leader. She got involved in voluntary work developing Asian women initiatives with the Barking Race Equality Council. In 1987 she joined the Barking and Dagenham Language Support Service as a bilingual support teacher and was promoted to co-ordinate the primary team of eleven teachers. Her work also entails substantial staff and curriculum development, as well as the production of learning material with parental involvement. She has also taught English as a Second Language to Asian Women at the Barking College of Technology. Rukhsana co-founded Cheetah Books, which publishes multicultural material for school children. She is a Member of the Board of Trustees of the QALB Centre, dealing with mental health issues and transcultural counselling.

In 1992 Rukhsana was appointed Justice of the Peace on the Barking Bench.

# Neelam Bakshi

Neelam Bakshi, an enthusiastic Latin American and Ballroom Dancer, runs her own training and management consultancy, NB Associates.

Neelam Bakshi

Born in Mombasa, Kenya, in 1960, Neelam has lived in Scotland since she was two. She studied Psychology and French at Glasgow University, after which she worked as a bookseller and training officer. She joined the Civil Service as a Revenue Executive and worked there for nine years before becoming a Development Officer with Strathclyde University, responsible for co-ordinating mentoring schemes. During this time Neelam became branch president of her union, and was a member of the Scottish TUC's Race Equality Committee.

Neelam has successfully participated in several training courses including workshops with leading practitioners in the personal development field. She holds a Practitioner Certificate in Neuro Linguistic Training (NLP), having trained with Richard Bandler (one of the co-founders of NLP) and McKenna Breen. As well as providing consultancy and training, Neelam runs courses in a range of areas including personal development and management and communication skills, as well as equal opportunities, a topic on which she has lectured at Glasgow and Strathclyde Universities.

Neelam was an elected member of Strathclyde Regional Council from 1990 until local government re-organisation in 1996. She chaired a number of committees, taking particular interest in youth, community development, and equality issues, including as a member of the Equal Opportunities Committee of the Convention of Scottish Local Authorities (COSLA). Her personal experiences of childhood abuse have been shared publicly and she has promoted facilities to empower women and children, including supporting the development of the Zero Tolerance Campaign against domestic violence.

As the first woman from a minority ethnic background ever elected as a councillor in Scotland, Neelam has had a strong profile on women's and racial equality issues, and won the Emily Award for her work in local government. However, she was unsuccessful in seeking nomination for a Parliamentary seat despite being shortlisted twice.

Neelam has been actively involved in the voluntary sector for many years, her advice being sought by a range of organisations including the Scottish Asian Action Committee, Meridian, Community Development Agency, the National Lotteries Charities Board (Scotland) Advisory Group, and the BBC Scotland Religious Advisory Group. She has served as a member of the John Wheatley Centre Policy Commission on Equal Opportunities in a Scottish Parliament.

Neelam has helped organise events for Save the Children, Children in Scotland, Scottish Education for Action and Development, and the Scottish Council for Voluntary Organisations and has been a regular contributor to BBC Radio Scotland's Thought for the Day.

Neelam is married with one daughter, She sees her work as helping to empower so that they might develop their own potential and have choices in creating their future.

## Anuradha Basu

Anuradha Basu

Anuradha Basu, a university lecturer, was born in Mumbai (Bombay), India, in 1960.

After graduating from the University of Delhi she obtained an MBA at the Indian Institute of Management in Calcutta, and came to Britain in 1986 to study at Cambridge University from where she earned a doctorate and an M Phil degree in economics.

Anuradha presently lectures in Management Studies and Economics at the University of Reading.

Her research interests include public finance, entrepreneurship and economic adjustment of enterprises in emerging market economies. She is the author of "Public Expenditure Decision Making: the Indian Experience".

Anuradha is currently directing a major research project on "South Asian entrepreneurship in Britain", funded by the Economic and Social Research Council which involves a study of 200 entrepreneurs of Bangladeshi, Indian and Pakistani origin, who own medium to large sized businesses in Britain. She is investigating the factors responsible for entrepreneurships among British Asians, their sources of finance, and the role community networks in influencing business survival and growth.

Anuradha is the mother of two children, aged eight and

three, and enjoys listening to Indian and Western Classical music, reading and walking.

# Shibani Basu

Born into a middle class joint family headed by her grandfather, Shibani Basu has delightful memories linked to her birth place, Mymensing. She and a cousin of the same age attended a local girls school, where they were given choices to participate in various sports, music and theatre.

Shibani Basu

Before she finished her schooling in Mymensing, her family moved to Calcutta just after partition. Shibani went on to complete her schooling at Monimala Girls School in Asansole, West-Bengal. Having a cousin who was a headmistress at the school. convinced Shibani that this was the perfect place for children to grow. After completing her schooling, she moved to Calcutta to continue further education and in 1960 obtained an Arts degree from Calcutta University. Always having the thrust for reading books and music, she joined a renowned music school in Calcutta and also attended a teachers' training course in 1961. Completing both courses in 1962, she embarked on her professional career by joining Ramkrishna Mission Institute of Culture Library in Calcutta as an Assistant Librarian. Whilst working, she also studied and obtained a Diploma in Librarianship from the University of Calcutta in 1964.

Arriving in Britain for further studies in 1966 resulted in marriage the same year to an accountant and commencement of employment as Assistant Librarian with London Borough of Brent. After three years, she joined the Borough of Enfield and, in 1975, the Borough of Wandsworth. With a wish to improve her career prospects, she studied and passed the Chartered Librarianship course of the Library Association of UK in 1976.

In 1986, she took up the post of Community Librarian for the Borough of Merton, where she is responsible for promoting library services within the Borough to ethnic minorities.

An elected committee member of Contour Housing Association and Milat Asian Housing Association, she was also Secretary of the Ethnic Community Centre in Vestry Hall, Mitcham, but had to relinquish these posts due to increased demand on her time to expand library services within the Borough. In order to attract more women to the library, Shibani formed "Asian Women Association", with the objective to encourage all women to take an active part in library activities and is honorary Chairperson. The organisation was one of the four projects short-listed out of 52 to receive the nation-wide Library Association/Holt Jackson Community Award in 1992.

Now an acting Vice-Chairperson of Co-operative of Indic Language Laser Authority, she attends periodic meetings as a specialist in Bengali language and is responsible for the cataloguing and classification of Bengali books.

She is also an active member of Asian Librarian and Officers' Groups and in her special interest for arts and crafts, she organises various exhibitions and social events as part of promoting library services.

# Ramini Baxi

Ramini Baxi

Ramini Baxi, the daughter of the celebrated Dr Major J.S. Chowan, was born in Bombay, India in 1946.

The product of the renowned Miranda College in New Delhi, she graduated with an MA in English and a MEd.

The first three years of her career were spent as a headmistress of a Secondary School in Kampala, East Africa. Arriving in Britain in 1968, she joined the Education Department in the borough of Newham, London.

Well known for her dedication and drive, as an Inset and Assessment co-ordinator, Ramini is also deeply involved in promoting awareness of Multiculturism in all spheres of education. With the exceptional commitment to bring about a synthesis of Oriental and Occidental cultures, and as a protagonist of Punjabi culture, many of the North Indian dances and programmes that she has organised have been presented to other schools.

Professional organiser and compere, who also enjoys writing poetry and singing classical and folk songs in Punjabi, Hindi and Urdu, Ramini has hosted numerous musical evenings for illustrious performers such as Jagjit Singh, Anup Jalota, Najma Aktar, and Surinder Kaur.

A physical-fitness enthusiast, Ramini has been involved in aerobics and yoga for the last twenty years. She lives with her husband Surjet, a Civil Engineer, a daughter who is doing law and a son who plans to become a dentist.

# Anita Bhalla

Born in Nairobi, Kenya, Anita Bhalla came to Britain with her family in 1964 and settled in Birmingham. After schooling, she qualify as a teacher with English as her main subject. During her college years, she was elected as a full-time official of the Students Union and was given a sabbatical year to carry out her duties. Whilst at college, she took on many issues of concern to students, including the lack of nursery facilities for women students, concerns of overseas students the fight against racism as well as general welfare and counselling work.

It was during her student days that Anita became concerned

about special injustice in the world and closer at home in Britain. After qualifying, she decided to work in the community and took up her first job in Leicester as a Community Relations Officer, where she worked giving general information and advice in particular to Asian and African Caribbean young people and women. It was in Leicester that she pioneered one of the first hostels for Asian women against much criticism from within the Asian community. The hostel become a valuable community resource and is still operating. She also co-authored a book for young people at this time.

From Leicester, she went on the Asian Resource Centre in Handsworth, Birmingham as a Community Worker with an additional responsibility for developing projects with Asian women and girls. While carrying out general casework and dealing with the issues arising from casework - housing, employment, social security, immigration and nationality, cultural and leisure provisions – she also established and managed a hostel for Asian women and worked as a home school liaison link.

Anita Bhalla

Her next link was as a lecturer with the Industrial Language Training Unit based in Walsall, teaching language and employment skills to industrial workers and planning and carrying out training in equal opportunities to employers in the private and public sector, and became a Senior Lecturer with regional responsibilities, co-ordinating training and staff development between six West Midland ILTUs.

Anita's career then took a major turn. While working as a lecturer she took up a hobby that led her into a broadcasting career. From being a presenter on a local BBC radio programme, she was taken on to present the first magazine programme in English aimed at the Asian community in Britain, Channel 4's Eastern Eye, whilst continuing with her radio presenting/ reporting. She also reported and presented BBC television's Asian Magazine. She took up a post with BBC Radio WM to set up, produce and develop programming for the Asian communities in the West Midlands. The service developed from just two hours to over 36 hours while she was Editor of the team and it is now part of the BBC Asian Network offering a full-time service. During this time, she made several one-off reports/documentaries for national radio and television. In 1992, she took up her current post as the first BBC Community Affairs Correspondent working to radio and television news programmes in the Midlands.

Throughout her life, Anita has maintained a strong commitment to public service and voluntary work. For many years she was Chair of Governors o a local multi-racial school. She was a member of the Commission on Social Justice. Currently the Chair of the Board at the ambitious Midlands Arts Centre and the Board of the Symphony Hall in Birmingham, she is part of the management support group to the Asian Resource Centre in Handsworth and a Patron of the pioneering University of the First Age (a Birmingham educational initiative designed to provide stimulating educational opportunities for children in secondary schools) as well as a trustee of the Community Development Foundation.

She has been the recipient of awards from many community groups and from the One World Broadcasting Trust. In 1996, she won the Television News Category at the 'Race in the Media Awards', organised by the Commission for Racial Equality, for her reporting of race issues in the Midlands.

# Zia Bhaloo

Zia Bhaloo was born in Tanzania in 1967 and came to England in 1980 to study Law at University College London, going on to qualify as a barrister.

In her spare time she enjoys walking, swimming, tennis and the theatre.

# Suman Bhargava

Suman Bhargava

Traditional in her outlook and a powerful motivating force behind her business, Suman Bhargava is founder of the Suman Marriage Bureau.

Born in Ajmer and brought up in Mathura, India she was encouraged by her parents to study, gaining a first class at the Kishori Raman Inter College, a BA and then eventually an MA in Hindi Literature from the Kishori Raman P.G. College, Agra University. While studying, Suman took time to indulge in her passion for music in Tabla, attaining the highest marks in instrumental music winning first prize in the Tabla Vadan and a first prize from Zilla Pardarshni Attawa, U.P.

After excelling as a public speaker and winning many awards, she was honoured with a first prize in debating from Akhil Bhartiya Sahkarta Saptah in 1959.

1964 was to be the year in which Suman married Rameshwar Nath Bhargava and the following year the couple migrated to Britain. In 1972, She established the Suman Marriage Bureau, as well as a Welfare Advisory Service. Since then Suman's career has been a success story littered with a whole array of awards and medals.

Committed to community and social work, Suman was invited to one of the Queen's garden parties for her outstanding work within the community. Her work with the Anti-Dowry Society won her the Mother India award, followed by the Mahilla Shiromani Award for keeping Asian Culture and

Tradition alive in the West, then the Pride of India Gold Medal Award. Her resumé was published in "The Best of British Women", 1993 and in 1995 she was awarded a trophy by the Punjabi Society of British Isles for her outstanding services to the community.

Suman values her friends highly which keeps her social life just as busy. She regularly takes part in Kavi Sammelans, cultural and religious events, enjoys reading and writing Hindi Poetry, watching Hindi films and listening to music.

# Usha Bhatt

Born and brought up in Kampala, Uganda, Usha Bhatt was sent to India at the age of 16 to study at Sophia College, Bombay and received a BA Honours Degree in History, Politics and Sociology.

Usha Bhatt

On returning to Kampala, she took up a post as teacher of History. Marriage to Charoovadan a dental surgeon was followed by the birth of her son and, while in Uganda, she was actively involved with the Ugandan Council of Women which undertook charitable work, helping deprived children and families, and the Indian Women's Association.

The family arrived in Britain in 1972, when Idi Amin expelled Asians from Uganda. Once settled and familiarised with the culture, Usha wanted to continue her voluntary work. She joined the Sangam Association of Asian Women in 1979 and was elected Secretary in 1980, Vice-President in 1982 and President in 1986, followed by re-election as President in 1995. Actively involved in helping Asians and the local community in various issues including domestic, marital, housing, immigration, legal, general problems and a wide range of cultural activities.

Usha is also involved in other Asian women' associations as well as in the field of social services.

Her interests include classical Indian music and dance, flower arranging and the art of bonsai.

# Zarina Bhimji

Zarina Bhimji, a talented artist was born in Uganda in 1963. At the age of nine her family emigrated to England permanently.

On leaving secondary school in 1981, Zarina studied foundation level Art at Leicester Polytechnic. Then in 1983 she joined Goldsmith's College at the University of London where she graduated with a Bachelor of Fine Arts. In 1989 Zarina completed her postgraduate studies at the notable Slade School of Fine Art, London. She also won the Coopers & Lybrand Award that year for the most outstanding work in any medium

- Zarina's medium being photography - by artists under the age of 35.

As a solo artist, Zarina has exhibited her work at many galleries around England including Goldsmith's College and Slade School of Art, the Tom Allen Community Art Centre, London, the Ikon Gallery, Birmingham and most recently Kettle's Yard, Cambridge University. Her work has also featured in group exhibitions world-wide since 1985, her most recent being at Guggenheim Museum in New York, the Walker Art Center, Minneapolis, Ulm Germany, South Johannesburg and Biennal, South Africa.

Zarina's work could be viewed as stylised, symbolic and highly diverse. She has successfully used photography, a medium which is continually having to prove itself as a art form, on a variety of subject matter, such as vital human organs, genocide and racism, bodies, hair, to paint a bigger picture on wide range of themes that she is interested. It is no wonder her work has been described as "both beautiful and frightening" and "remarkable and disturbing".

As well as being reviewed by over 38 newspaper and magazines since 1982, she has been interviewed by BBC television and radio. She also has collections in private galleries and museums in London and Germany. She published *"Illuminations Television"* on CDROM, incorporating work from the Rencontres au Noir project in 1995.

Zarina is currently working as a lecturer at the London College of Printing and spends her free time cooking, travelling and being with people who mean a lot to her.

# Sudha Bhuchar

The actress Sudha Bhuchar was born and brought up in East Africa and India and has lived in England for over twenty years.

Her career developed by accident. Sudha was lured to Tara Arts as a teenager and caught the "acting bug". She turned professional in 1983 after graduating with a BA in Math/Sociology from London University. She has since appeared on stage, television and radio, including on Channel 4's feature drama Turning World.

Sudha participated in the Royal Court International Summer School in 1995 as a writer. She turned to writing because "there are no good parts for the thirty-something women". She co-authored a four part radio drama broadcast on Radio 4, Girlies with Shaheen Khan.

Sudha Bhuchar

She has played Meena in Eastenders, Kiran Bedi in Family Pride and the glamourous icon in Memsahib Rita a drama made for the BBC.

In 1989 she set up Tamasha Theatre company with Kristine

Landon-Smith.

Tamasha's acclaimed East Is East was probably the first Asian production to be performed in London's West End.

Sudha has produced and acted in other plays by Tamasha including A Shaft of Sunlight, Women of the Dust, Untouchable and House of the Sun directed by Kristine Landon-Smith.

Other theatre credits include The Broken Thigh and The Little Clay Cart, by Jatinder Verma; Romeo and Juliet by Anthony Clark; Torpedoes in the Jacuzzi by Phil Young; and Prem by James McDonald.

Sudha has presented Network East, an Asian Magazine programme from BBC Pebble Mill, Birmingham.

She played Usha Gupta on BBC Radio 4's The Archers, Becoming the first ever Asian person to appear in a long running series about an English rural community.

# Illa Bhuva

Illa Bhuva, a Secretary and Community Worker was born in 1946 in Gujarat, India.

After completing a secretarial course with bookkeeping and computing, Illa worked with the Indian High Commission for twelve years while in Nairobi, Kenya.

In 1975 she came to Britain and spent her spare time doing voluntary work. Then in 1991 she joined the UK Asian Women's Conference as a voluntary Secretary. Since then she has worked as a Chair lady and has successfully established several projects and schemes to help the Asian community in general and specifically Asian women.

Illa has also attained a diploma in Interpreting and Translation and successfully completed a Basic Skills Counselling course.

At present she holds the post of Honorary Secretary and helps organise activities and projects for Asian women.

# Malkiat Bilku
# and the Hillingdon Strikers

Malkiat Bilku is the Shop Steward of 53 strikers at Hillingdon Hospital.

The strikers, mainly Asian domestic and catering workers, were sacked by a private company, Pall Mall, in October 1995 for refusing to accept a 20% pay cut.

Their 20 month long strike is not only about better working

Malkiat Bilku and the Hillingdon Strikers

conditions but also in defence of the National Health Service. Despite facing racist abuse and arrest on the picket line, the strikers are resolute in their struggle. Their union, UNISON, after initially supporting the strike, stopped paying strike pay in January 1997.

Malkiat and other strikers regularly attend meetings all over the country and abroad, raising finance and support for their cause. With determination and motivation from each other, the strikers will continue their struggle until all 53 are reinstated on their previous pay and work conditions.

# Chitraleka Bolar

Chitraleka Bolar, a renowned Bharatanatyam dancer and choreographer, was born in Kerala, India 1956.

Chitraleka was trained from a young age by Sri Mohan Kumar and Guru Rajaratnam Pillai. Since her arrival in England in 1978 Chitraleka has been at the forefront of teaching Bharatanatyam in this country.

Her love for dance and her dedication to teaching Bharatanatyam resulted in her producing the first generation of dancers to be trained professionally in this country. Not content for dance enthusiasts to come to her, Chitraleka has taken workshops and performances to schools and community centres all over Britain. In many rural areas of Britain her work has not just been an introduction to Indian dance but also the children's first insight to Indian culture.

Concentrating on her solo performances from 1978 to 1989, she then choreographed for the Lasya Dance Company, performing duets with dancers such as Nahid Siddiqui. In 1995 Chitraleka researched Kaishiki – a dance form based on Baratanatyam with live music, then, in 1996, along with Roger Sinha, she developed Kaishiki and toured with their production Visions of Rhythm.

Through her dance company "Chitraleka and Company," Chitraleka strives to create innovative and stimulating work rooted in the Bharatanatyam tradition and seeks to develop Bharatanatyam in a contemporary context in this country.

# Gurdeep Kaur Chadha

Gurdeep Kaur Chadha, daughter of a well-known successful businessman, was born and brought up in Nairobi, Kenya where she had a very happy and privileged childhood. At the age of 12, Gurdeep went to boarding school in Masoori, India, where she completed her 'O' levels. Having a strong desire to study science, she returned to Nairobi to complete her 'A' levels and continued her education at the University of Nairobi, where she gained a degree in Botany and Zoology followed by a Masters in Entomology. Awarded with a scholarship, she went on to post-graduate research at the famous Agricultural Institute in Wageningen, Holland.

Returning to Nairobi in 1972, Gurdeep worked for the International Centre for Insect Physiology and Ecology. She married a successful lecturer and scientist Dr Darminder Sirsh (who was awarded an MBE) in 1973, and they both came to the UK for permanent settlement.

Gurdeep Kaur Chadha

Gurdeep worked for the Overseas Development Administration. During this period she published Scientific papers and completed a Diploma Course in Electron Microscopy at Thames University. When Darminder got a job in Yorkshire, Gurdeep followed him with a job at the British Lending Library at Boston Spa.

A career break came when she had two daughters but, whilst bringing them up, Gurdeep did voluntary work with the Women's Royal Voluntary Service and with the Racial Equality Council. The work with the Racial Equality Council in York involved helping the Ugandan refugee settlers with language problems and eliminating racial discrimination in the remote parts of North Yorkshire.

Gurdeep started teaching Indian Cookery to adults at night school and during this time was appointed the first Asian woman magistrate for the York bench in North Yorkshire.

In 1984, she returned to work for a private Biotechnological company based at York University.

An active committee member of the charity York Against Cancer, she helped organise fund-raising activities.

Since 1990 she has been involved in the International Hemkunt Foundation which promotes Sikh history and culture amongst children.

With constant support and encouragement from her husband and two daughters, she successfully combines a happy family life with work and spare time activities of travelling, walking and climbing. Along with her family she has climbed Mount Snowdon, Hemkunt peak of the Himalayas and Mount Kenya and regularly walks in the Yorkshire Dales, Yorkshire Moors and the Lake District.

# Gurinder Chadha

Providing a serious insight into the life of the Asian communities with a touch of humour, Gurinder Chadha is the film director of Bhaji on the Beach.

Born in Nairobi, Kenya, Gurinder arrived in Britain at the tender age of two. She went on to attain a BA in Development

Studies and a Post Graduate Diploma in Broadcasting.

Starting her working life as a news reporter with the BBC, Gurinder moved on to direct several award-winning documentaries for the British Film Institute, the BBC and Channel 4. Her first drama was a Short Film for Channel 4 called A Nice Arrangement which was then selected for Critics Week in Cannes in 1991.

Gurinder Chadha

Through her first feature film, Gurinder has now received world-wide recognition for her directorial skills. The film Bhaji on the Beach has won countless international awards, including the Audience's favourite film at Locarno and Brisbane. Bhaji on the Beach was nominated for Best British Film at the BAFTAs. Gurinder personally was voted the Best Newcomer in the 1994 Evening Standard British Film Awards. Its a notable fact that "Bhaji was part of a recent group of Channel 4 films that have led to a resurgence in New British Cinema".

In 1995 Gurinder directed a two-part drama set in working-class Liverpool for BBC1 called Rich Deceiver, watched by 11 million viewers and has recently co-written the screen play Thanksgiving Day - a humourous and poignant view of contemporary American life similar to that of "Bhaji". As a director of growing stature, she has been invited as a guest lecturer to several US universities, presenting papers on her work in Britain.

Hollywood producer, Susan Cartsouis, has optioned a book for Gurdiner to adapt and direct through her Disney-backed company Wind dancer Films.

Gurinder is also making her first British Bollywood movie this Summer with an all star Bollywood cast with British Asian actors. The film is entitled London and is set here.

Gurinder's goal is to live life to the full, exploiting the huge advantages of being part of the Indian Diaspora which includes music, film, clothes, food and all other forms of creativity.

# Tochi Chaggar

Tochi Chaggar, a television personality in Kenya and a veteran of Asian radio in Britain was born in 1944 and brought up in Kenya, East Africa. Whilst still at school aged 15, she was hired as a continuity announcer on Kenyan radio, after her singing voice had been heard on air and noticed by those with influence. After completing her studies she went on to full-time work in television as a production assistant and was later promoted to the ranks of producer/ director, thus becoming the only Asian woman in television production in the country.

Married to a popular television and radio personality Pretam Singh Chagger, in 1970 when her career was at its peak, to devote time to her family. In 1986, seeking a better education of her children, she came to Britain without her husband. The family split was such a struggle, however, that it resulted in a complete and permanent transfer of residence for the whole family.

Shortly after arriving in Britain, she resumed her long association with Asian radio by obtaining a Sunday slot on Sina radio. She has played a key role in the campaign for the first ever licensed ethnic radio station 'Sunrise Radio'. After working for a few years with Sunrise radio, she moved on to Spectrum radio where she co-hosted a ground breaking afternoon slot with colleague Parveen Muirzah, discussing pressing topical and often taboo subject matters such as wife beating, divorce, second marriages and step children. This programme played a crucial role in boosting the confidence of Asian women in Britain.

In spite of her success as a media personality, Tochi prefers to remain out of the spotlight. Her leisure hours are spent quietly with books, music - ghazals being her "hidden passion" or watching 'art' films.

# Qudsia Chandran

Dr Qudsia Chandran was born in Mardan, in the North West Frontier Province of Pakistan to Muslim parents. Educated in Predentation Convent School, Peshawar, she qualified as a doctor from Fatima Jinnah Medical College, Lahore, the only women's medical college in Pakistan. She went on to work in hospitals in Lahore, Peshawar and Kohat before coming to England. It was here that Qudsia met and married her husband, Raj, a Tamil from Sri Lanka.

Qudsia Chandran

In 1967 Qudsia worked in Doncaster Royal Infirmary where she took her DRCOG qualification. The following year she began general practice and in 1969 was appointed as Principal General Practitioner in Sutton-In-Ashfield, Nottinghamshire in partnership with her husband. In 1970 she was appointed as Family Planning Medical Officer.

During this period, Qudsia helped her husband win District Council elections as Councillor in Ashfield and was involved in advising the Nottingham branch of All Pakistan's Women's Association on health matters concerning Pakistani women. In 1977 she was elected Social Secretary of North Trent Division of the Overseas Doctors' Association and in 1987 organised the Asian Women's National Conference in London where several Ministers of State were invited to speak on national matters and those concerning women.

Qudsia has been involved in a number of events concerning the Conservative Party - helping her husband fight as a Conservative parliamentary candidate in the 1987 General Election and speaking on the Health Debate at the Conservative

Party Conference in Brighton to over 4000 delegates. In 1992 she was invited to join the East Midlands Area Conservative Women's Committee and as spokesperson for One Nation Forum. The following year, she was invited to propose a motion on Health at the National Women's Conference in London and to join the Blue Ribbon Committee by the Conservative Party.

In June 1994, Qudsia and her husband were joined by Rt Hon Virginia Bottomley JP MP, the Secretary of State for Health, to celebrate 25 years of uninterrupted general practice together. In the same year, she organised a National Reception for Asian ladies to meet the Secretary of State for Health.

In October 1996, Qudsia was elected as one of the Women of The Year and invited to celebrate this at a Lunch at The Savoy, London.

In May 1997, she was elected as Vice-Chairman of the, Overseas Doctors Association, North Trent Division. She was also elected as the Vice-Chairman of Sherwood Conservative Women's Committee. Qudsia is a member of Conservative Medical Society and British Medical Association.

# Debjani Chatterjee

Debjani Chatterjee, Writer, Storyteller and Educationalist now living and working in Sheffield, was born in Delhi in 1952.

Debjani Chatterjee

Given the Dean's Honour Roll and the President's Scholarship at the American University in Cairo, she moved to England in 1972 to continue her studies, attaining a Masters, PhD and a PGCE.

Debjani's career began as a lecturer in Comparative Religion at Didsbury College of Education, Manchester. In the following two years she was awarded Senate Studentship at the University of Lancashire and came out of the academic field to work as an Export Sales Assistant and Sector Manager for the British Steel Corporation in Rotherham and Sheffield.

Returning to teaching in 1981, her first assignment was at the Chaucer Secondary School in Sheffield and later as the Head of Religious Education at Park House Secondary, Sheffield.

In 1984, she became the Principal Community Relations Officer for the Sheffield Racial Equality Council where she worked for ten years. During this time she won various prizes for her writing, at The Lancaster Literature Festival Poetry Competition, Peterloo Poets Open Poetry Competition, Raymond Williams Community Publishing Prize, Southport Writers' Circle Poetry Competition, Yorkshire and Humberside Arts Writers Award and a Women in the Arts Travel Award. Her book 'The Elephant-Headed God and

Other Hindu Tales was selected for Children's Books of the Year.

In 1985, Debjani co-founded a Bengali Women's Support Group, of which she became Chairperson in 1995.

Working as the Director of Oxfordshire Racial Equality Council in 1994, she also became a member of the government's Inner Cities Religious Council and was elected to the council of the Poetry Society.

Currently working as a Co-ordinator of the Distance Learning Project in Sheffield, she is also a member of the Arts Council Literature Panel.

Integrating her love of creativity and academia, she is a keen cartoonist and community developer and enjoys stamp collecting.

# Anuradha Roma Choudhury

Anuradha Roma Choudhury was born in Calcutta in 1939.

She studied at the University of Calcutta attaining her BA in Sanskrit and MA in Sanskrit Literature. Awarded a Gold medal for her Gita-bharati Degree in Indian music, she sang a duet with the legendary Hemanta Mukherjee in the Bengali film 'Alor pipasa' in 1963.

Anuradha Roma Choudhury

Roma arrived in England in 1970 with her husband Dr Bishnupada Pal Choudhury, a doctor and lecturer at the University of Wales in Cardiff. She completed her PGCE in Cardiff while bringing up her young family - daughter Purba and son Pushaun.

She began work as a part-time tutor with the Department of Continuing Education of the University of Wales and continues to lecture extensively on topics related to Indian music, customs, family life and Hinduism.

In 1987, she published a book on Indian music and in 1988 contributed to the book 'The Essential Teachings of Hinduism', edited by Kerry Brown Rider. In the same year, a half-hour programme was made by HTV Wales on 'A Week in the Life of Roma Choudhury' and in 1994 she contributed to the series 'Themes in Religious Studies', edited by Jean Holm Pinter.

Currently a Librarian in charge of the Asian Language section at Cardiff County Library Services, she writes occasional articles for Bengali magazines based in Calcutta and plays an active role in several Asian, Interfaith and Multicultural organisations.

Roma is an accomplished singer and a teacher of Indian vocal music. She also enjoys floor painting from Bengal, a topic for which she organises workshops in schools and during festivals.

# Purba Choudhury

Purba Choudhury

Purba Choudhury was born in Calcutta, India and brought up in Wales. Educated at Cardiff High School, where she was Head Girl and a member of the Board of Governors in 1985/86, she went on to graduate from St Hilda's College, University of Oxford with a BA in Psychology, Philosophy and Physiology in 1990 and had an MA (Oxon) conferred in 1995.

She began working for the City of Oxford Orchestra as the Marketing and Publicity Officer and as a Press and Publicity Officer for the Royal Liverpool Philharmonic Society the following year. Since 1993, she has been working as a Press and Information Officer at the London Arts Board.

In 1995 Purba presented a series of eight music programmes for BBC Radio 2.

Musically multi-talented, she has sung with a jazz quartet, the Royal Liverpool Philharmonic Choir and South Glamorgan Youth Choir, the Welsh National Opera Children's Chorus. She also plays classical western pianoforte and improvises jazz and dances Bharatanatyam, Jazz and Contemporary, Ballroom and Lindy Hop.

Amongst her other interests are ayurvedic and other alternative health therapies, yoga and reading.

# Rashmi Choudhury

Rashmi Choudhury

Rashmi Choudhury was born in London on 4th July 1973. Her parents instilled in her the values of working and playing hard and independent thoughts free of prejudice. Rashmi was always close to her two brothers, the eldest of whom is autistic.

A keen sportsperson, Rashmi won her school sports prize five years in a row. For fourteen years she trained as an ice skater every morning form 5am - 8am before school and competed all over the country and abroad.

In 1994, after gaining a BSc Joint Honours Degree in Media and the Social Sciences, Rashmi decided to pursue her ambition to raise funds and awareness for the National Autistic Society which supports the 115,000 families in the UK affected by autism. She did this by bungee-jumping (twice) 300 ft from the Chelsea Bridge Tower in London.

At the age of 23, Rashmi was involved in her first legal case, against a builder who had carried out unsatisfactory work on a property she has purchased in Norfolk. She won the case.

In 1995, Rashmi accepted a place at Cambridge University, where she completed a thesis examining the treatment methods available to people with autism for which she was awarded her MPhil. During her time at University, Rashmi joined the Women's Ice Hockey Team, winning a half blue for her effort in a Varsity game against Oxford. She also took part in rowing, running and joined the Officer's Training Corps. The OTC encouraged leadership and courage and Rashmi was one of the two women in her year to join the infantry wing. Rashmi then gained entry to the Royal Military Academy Sandhurst to train as an officer. However, she decided against a military career.

In 1997 Rashmi ran in the London Marathon for the National Autistic Society and joined the Territorial Army. She remains actively engaged in fundraising for the National Autistic Society.

# Maya Chowdhry

Maya Chowdhry, who considers herself mainly a "self taught" artist is a freelance playwright and poet.

Born of an Indian father and British mother in Edinburgh, 1964, she draws upon her own experiences and her duel identity. Combining words with images, Maya gained an MA in Scriptwriting for Film and Television from the Leeds Metropolitan University. Her talents were further developed in writer's workshops. She is heavily influenced by what is around her, in the street, in the sky, on television. With her eyes wide open, she is influenced as much by what she sees and what she doesn't see and thus her reason for writing is "to have a voice".

Maya Chowdhry

The written word is not the only tool Maya uses to express her ideas. Also working as a film-maker, photographer, and performance poet she has toured extensively with her performances, including performing "Beyond" and "Monsoon" at the Highways Performance Space, in Los Angeles, "The Sacred House" in two consecutive years (1993-1994) at the Institute of Contemporary Arts and the National Review of Live Art respectively. BBC Radio were quick to pick up on her talent, broadcasting several of her plays such as "The Heart and Heaven" and most recently "Samsara". "Kaahini" will be touring with the Red Ladder Theatre Company.

Maya's poetry has been published on numerous occasion by a plethora of publications and awards are not an uncommon feature. She won her first prize for "Monsoon" in the BBC Radio Drama Young Playwrights Festival, 1991 and in 1992 "Brides of Dust" won first prize at the Cardiff International Poetry Competition. In 1993 "Death Rites" was the winner of the Littlewood Arc Short Story Competition and in 1994, the Arts Council gave her a Resident Dramatist Grant for the Red Ladder Theatre Company.

Maya has also been involved in writing workshops and residencies for a number of years.

Maya's belief is to project a positive and challenging image of women. Her themes range from racism to reincarnation but always come back to the mysteries of life

# Jagjit Chuhan

Jagjit Chuhan

Jagjit Chuhan is an artist for whom painting is a "means of self-realisation" of "becoming". Her paintings and drawings chart a spiritual voyage, "acknowledging a state of enslavement as a woman and degrees of empowerment through action".

Her work focuses on real-life experiences which exist parallel to and are interconnected with the ideal. The main Theme of her paintings is to explore the aspirations of women and men; the necessity to live through the various stages of one's life before acquiring the mental space to be creative, and the way this process is aided by mythical stories which interplay with contemporary life.

Jagjit's self portraits, which were exhibited at the Usher Gallery in Lincoln, assert her own identity as a female artist in relationship with other sculptures, paintings and life experiences.

She trained at the Slade School in London in the 70's and has won considerable recognition for her work, including an Arts Council Award for research into Indian Art in 1988, a Production Award from North West Arts Board in 1995, and a Research Fellowship from Liverpool John Moores University in 1995. Jagjit has been involved in numerous projects and collaborations since 1983, including her giving public lectures and implementing practical workshops.

Her art has been widely exhibited including at the Tate Gallery, Liverpool in 1990, Galeria Civica in Marsala, Italy in 1991, Arnolfini Gallery, Bristol in 1992, Museum of Women's Art, London and Birmingham Museum and Art Gallery in 1994, and at Kapil Jariwala Gallery, London in 1996.

Jagjit is currently working on a series of paintings focusing on portraiture within a narrative and symbolic context, mainly of women, under the collective title 'Powerful Women – Changing Conventions'. In addition she is curating an exhibition on the subject of drawing, looking at universal and culture-specific aesthetics in drawing in the visual arts and education.

At present Jagjit is a Fine Art Lecturer at Liverpool Art School, John Moores University.

Shama Contractor

# Shama Contractor

Shama Contractor whose teaching career spans over 40 years was born in Baroda in 1924. Beginning her career in Bombay as the head of a large Muslim girls school, she went on to head an Urdu primary school in the Education department of Bombay Municipal Corporation. Since her arrival in England in 1966 until her retirement in 1994, Shama taught at various schools in Hackney.

With her strong interest in all issues relating to women's welfare, Shama co-founded and was the chair of Asian Women's Refuge, a safe house for battered wives in Waltham Forest.

Presently the chair and founder member, she also runs the Muslim Women's Welfare Association (MWWA).

Shama feels that if women are given adequate support and advice, it can help them to look at the realistic choices they may have and enable them to take steps to achieve them.

With social and women's issues at the forefront of her work, Shama tries her utmost to help those who approach her with personal problems either directly or through her organisation.

# Sarla Coonar

Sarla Coonar, an Orthodontist, was born in Gujranwala, Pakistan in 1935. Sarla commenced her career in India as an Assistant Professor in Dental Surgery at Madras Medical College and later as an Assistant Surgeon for the Dental Surgery at Irwin Hospital in Delhi. She left India for permanent settlement in Britain in 1968.

She now works as Principal in a Specialist Orthodontist Practice in Barnet, Hertfordshire and employs 13 people including two part-time dental surgeons and a part-time consultant oral surgeon.

She enjoys vocal Hindustani classical singing and is a member of the Inner Wheel Rotary Club of Mill Hill London.

# Shirley Miriam Daniel

Shirley Miriam Daniel, whose long and successful teaching career spans nearly forty years, was born in Madras in 1935.

She began her path to a career in education by gaining a BSc BT at Madras University, becoming the Head of Physics and Mathematics at the Convent of Jesus and Mary in Delhi.

Arriving in Britain in 1965, she taught in Scotland before coming to London in 1969. Three years later she was appointed as Head of Science, from which the natural progression was Chief Examiner of Science for CSE, then Chief Examiner of GCSE Science. Since 1993 she has been the Chief Examiner of GNVQ in Science.

Shirley Miriam Daniel

Taking a slight change of direction in 1986 Shirley became Headteacher of a large secondary school. Now retired Shirley is an Inspector of schools for OFSTED and an Education Consultant.

Having a high profile on educational issues, Shirley has also focused on Black and Asians in management issues. She is serving as a member of the Ethnic Minorities Advisory

Committee to the Judicial Studies Board.

A Non-Executive Director of the North Thames Regional Health Authority moving to the same post in Brent and Harrow Regional Health Authority in 1996, she is currently a member of ICSTIS - Independent Committee for the Supervision of Telecommunication and Information Services - the Windsor Fellowship Advisory Council, and a trustee of Anne Frank Educational Trust and Citizenship Foundation.

Life is not all work, for when Shirley finds time, she enjoys quiet walks, travelling, singing and playing bridge.

# Jayaben Desai

Jayaben Desai is known as the lady behind the epic Grunwick strike.

Jayaben Desai

Born into a business family in India in 1933, Jayaben's early schooling was truncated as family responsibilities intervened as a result of her mother's illness. However, she later secured a qualification in dressmaking.

She and her husband moved to England in 1968. While bringing up her two sons, Jayaben used her creative skills by dressmaking from home.

Later she joined the Grunwick photo processing factory in north London as a part-time worker soon moving on to become a full-timer. Jayaben was one of 12 Asian women working at the firm, all of whom accepted the poor working conditions because they did not know any different.

Jayaben supported her fellow workers, who like her, were pressurised into working excessive overtime. For this, she incurred the displeasure of her employer, who, one evening called her into his office and subjected her to a verbal abuse. Jayaben eventually stormed out of his office. Her elder son, who was working at the factory as a summer job, threw his own card on the floor and followed his mother out of the building.

Discussing the incident at home that evening, her husband suggested that they create their own union or become part of one. Not knowing where to go or who to see, Jayaben and her son were directed to APEX by Brent Trades Council. Thus the epic Grunwick strike was triggered. Continuing for more than a year, it displayed the industrial militancy of Asian women to the world.

Engrossed in the cause throughout the strike, Jayaben did not stop to think about her tiny 4' 10" frame as she stood up to numerous over 6' tall. At one time, a quarter of the Metropolitan Police was mobilised to counter the Grunwick picket line. Fighting for what was right and believing in her own strength, Jayaben refused to be ignored or brushed aside.

Today, Jayaben is a voluntary worker at Kenmoor Park

Community Centre, where assists in a range of teaching activities, from yoga and acupressure to Asian culture.

# Indra Lavinia Deva

Indra Lavinia Deva, a demonstrably supportive individual, completed her schooling in Mauritius and arrived in England in 1970, where she started her own boutiques specialising in a wool shop and designer clothes.

Indra Lavinia Deva

After her son started his schooling at Eton College, Indra had more time to devote to her businesses. When in 1987 her husband was selected to fight for the Hammersmith constituency, Indra spent time on the campaign trail. In 1991, when her husband was selected to fight the Hounslow, Brentford, Isleworth and Chiswick constituency, Indra sold her shops to spend time helping him in his campaign. It was fortunate that she did so because the recession had just started. After her husband's election as the first Asian Conservative MP this century, Indra decided to work closely with him as his secretary at the House of Commons. This gave her a fascinating insight into the 'Corridors of Power', seeing how things really work; what is possible and what is not; who actually calls the shots in Government and how busy an MPs life really is. It came as a big shock to her to realise that her husband works 90 hours a week on average, both in the Commons, on his Constituency affairs, his work as a PPS to the Scottish Office and as a Deputy Lord Lieutenant of Greater London.

Indra is now Chairman of a Ward, Patron of the Women's Conference in Brentford and Isleworth. She was vice president of the Conservative Party's Winter Ball which was chaired by Mrs Gillian Clarke, wife of the then Chancellor of the Exchequer, and is also on the committee of the Blue Ball.

Indra has recently finished writing 'Mrs Deva's Cook Book' which brings together all the recipes of the Asian Community.

Assisting her husband with his work was more than a full-time job, but Indra still squeezed in the time to launch a campaign to help asthma sufferers who are increasing in numbers because of pollution.

She enjoys entertaining immensely and spending time with her family, especially with her elderly mother who now needs care and attention. A keen traveller, cook and theatre-goer, she is also the proud owner of two poodles, Bijou, who opened Crufts in 1995, and Bonzo, his playful brother.

# Hema Devlukia

Born in Uganda in 1956 into a family with a wealth of values and educational aspirations, Hema Devlukia was brought up and studied up to 'O' level standard on a small sugar estate in Uganda, where life seemed utopic.

Arriving in Britain as a Ugandan refugee in 1972, she was traumatised by the experience of being a refugee in Britain. Thanks to her parents' commitment to education, particularly for a daughter, she continued her 'A' levels in a number of RAF camps where refugees were housed by the British Government and eventually qualified BSc in Applied Microbiology from Strathclyde University in Glasgow.

Hema Devlukia

Her childhood was influenced by her father who was very patriotic with Gandhian philosophies (equal rights for women and minority groups), an ex-freedom fighter with strong views on the British empire and rule in India. The work her parents did with untouchables in Bombay, addressing issues of poverty, education and life skills also has a lasting influence. It was not surprising, therefore, that she was attracted to a career in the National Health Service, focusing mainly on the minority groups who were disadvantaged either by gender or race in accessing Eurocentric health services.

In 1993, having moved to London and married Sailesh, she was appointed on a joint project of the Department of Health and Save the Children Fund as a campaign assistant, to access and develop care for Asian women across England. This involved her in influencing maternity services strategies developed by the Department of Health and Maternity alliance.

This two year experience invoked her interest in women's health and subsequently she went on to specialise in issues focusing on women's health with a special interest in middle-aged women and health service provision for their needs.

Her passion for women's health led her to exploring health in a holistic mode: empowerment, community development, assertiveness and self esteem. This dimension was essential in an NHS dominated by male physicians and decision makers. She continued working in health promotion, however, this time developing holistic care packages for women in the area of menopause, breast and cervical cancer, sexual health and female genital mutilation. She subsequently became a freelance trainer with the Workers Educational Association in the spare time she had between her career, children and social and family commitments.

Having worked on women's issues, the next obvious link was employment and the juggling terms of employment, and their role as a wife and a mother. This led to the arena of developing Equal Opportunity Policies for a number of statutory organisations, with the main focus being black and minority ethnic women who are often in triple jeopardy due to gender, race and marital status.

In 1994, having attended a fast track management course for women in the NHS, she was appointed at a senior management level with a health authority addressing, at a strategic level, the commissioning role of health authorities in providing services to the black and minority ethnic groups in West London.

She continues to be committed to women's health and, in her spare time, works for a number of organisations supporting and empowering women in accessing health services.

Having had two daughters, her interest in child development grew. Her interaction with the education system led her to becoming a school governor where she had the opportunity of influencing the planning and delivery of education for children.

Having turned 40 and seeing her parents turn into older members of society, her interest turned to the social and health needs of older people, in particular women who are often the main carers in the society. She was actively involved in campaigning for the rights of Asian elders in the community care plans developed jointly by the health and local authorities.

Despite the above commitments, she finds time for her mental and physical relaxation, participating in many sports activities, as well as persevering with her interests in alternative therapy by obtaining a degree in Aromatherapy.

# Navdeep K Dhaliwal

Born in Glasgow in 1977, Navdeep Dhaliwal is from a sporting family, especially on her father's side, although her mother's brother was a cyclist who competed at national level.

When Navdeep first got involved with athletics it was simply to improve her general level of fitness. She had no intention of ever competing in sport beyond the level of school sports day, even though it was what she dreamed of but, thought it was an unrealistic ambition.

Navdeep K Dhaliwal

Navdeep trained seven days a week all year round to build her fitness at the age of 10. She worked closely with her parents as only they understood how hard she needed to train. Later she started training with her local club, City of Glasgow AC, but is now a member of Shaftesbury Barnett AC which is based in London. Working with endurance coaches, Navdeep competed in cross countries for a season. Due to her height and build, she progressed more rapidly in the throws, eventually winning at her school sports day and then competing for her club throughout the summer. Her father, a former discus thrower, was able to coach her.

Navdeep has represented Scotland in 11 internationals in shot putt and discus. She holds two Scottish national and two Scottish school records in shot putt. In 1992 she was the British shot putt Champion in Under 15 and ranked second in Discus. In the same year, Navdeep was awarded the UK Women's League Junior Athlete of the Year.

One of the highlights of Navdeep's athletic career so far was the award Francis Barker shield for the most meritorious performances in Scottish School Girl's Championships, after breaking the 13 year old shot putt record.

In 1993-94 Navdeep, a member of the Great Britain junior squad was selected for the World Schools Championships held in Cyprus. She has been captain of the Scotland team for the Celtic Games and a captain of school athletics team. In 1996 Navdeep received a bronze medal in shot putt in the British Universities.

Due to her commitment and her parents support throughout the initial years, Navdeep realised her ambition and potential in sport. Her parents still continue to support her, which she feels is just as important as all those years ago.

Currently a student in her second year of a Bachelor of Dental Surgery at Glasgow University, she hopes to continue her athletics career and represent Great Britain sometime in the near future.

# Spinder Dhaliwal

Spinder Dhaliwal

"Success smells sweet and makes inspiring reading too" reckons Spinder Dhaliwal, author of Profile of Five Asian Entrepeneurs.

Born in 1964 and arriving in Britain at the tender age of 3, she graduated in Economics and continued with academics until she completed her PhD. She took to researching Asian business and became increasingly convinced that business was certainly one area where Asians had proved themselves very successful.

A freelance journalist specialising in articles on business and education, she was no alien to writing. Looking for an answer to the question "there must be an easier way to make money in business" which had nagged her since she watched her father work long and hard in the news agency he owned, was the inspiration behind the book.

"I wanted to pursue the success of the Asian community, something they could be proud of, play down the negative aspects and portray Asians with dignity and respect" confirms the senior lecturer of Business Studies.

Her book traces the background of five extraordinarily successful UK businesses set up by Asian entrepeneurs and charts the development of each business, its operational and marketing strategies and future plans.

Spinder's personal plan for the future is, inevitably to write another book. This time she wants to focus purely on the female Asian entrepreneur, intrigued by the fact that so few Asian women own businesses themselves.

A lot of women, she feels, run a major part of a business from managing the paperwork to planning publicity, yet it is always the father, brother or husband who actually own it. "Why so?" is the next question which nags her!

# Harjinder Kaur Dhanjil

Born and brought up in Kenya, Harjinder Kaur Dhanjil came to England as a young bride in 1984. Although full of anticipation and dreams, she found the life and culture here different but her new life stretched her spiritual and religious beliefs.

Harjinder Kaur Dhanjil

It took time for her to adjust to the culture. Firstly she began to help her husband with business and then the children came along and slowly England became home with friends and family. She found that her husband has been very supportive and her real strength. Armed with new confidence and with her natural female housekeeping skills, cost budgeting and watching the bottom line, she was pleased to spot a business opportunity with Oriflame, a skincare company which sells natural products.

Two years later she is a Premier Executive in this firm, successfully managing a strong team of girls all over England, who in turn have their own teams and are growing from strength to strength. Climbing up the success ladder within the company has been fun and hard work but the rewards have been enormous.

This network selling has given her the opportunity to help other women build up confidence and start up from small beginnings.

As well as running her business successfully, Harjinder strongly believes in home and family life. If her children are to play a full part in society and not be exploited, they will need to know their rights and entitlements as well as their obligations to others, so instilling a sense of duty and responsibility is an essential part of their upbringing.

Despite her busy lifestyle, she is a member of many organisations where she works as a volunteer, especially with 'Jaago' Punjabi Women's group. Traditional in her outlook and beliefs, she sees accepting change and moving forward as part of life.

Her compassion and loyalty to friends and those who look to her for help is assured and her sense of humour, despite being exposed to the harshness of life, remains intact.

# Jaya Dheer

Jaya Dheer, born in 1942 and brought up in Bombay, is a highly sought after dance teacher, director, and workshop leader of Bharatanatyam.

At the tender age of eight, Jaya became a Bharatanatyam

Jaya Dheer

student with Acharya Parvati Kumar, where her talent and dedication for the art form became apparent and the path to her career was decided. Her early work won her recognition and numerous state awards. Jaya was regularly honoured with invitations by the government of Maharastra to perform in national and international dance and music festivals in India and abroad.

By the 1970s Jaya was studying under the auspices of the famous guru Padmshree Kelucharan Mahapatra. Shortly afterwards she married Kathak exponent Sudharshan Dheer. In 1977 Jaya founded the Abhinaya Darpan Academy in Bombay, Its primary aim was to promote India's immensely rich and varied culture throughout India and abroad. Since it's conception the academy has successfully undertaken countless tours around India and abroad with their productions based on the great Indian epics.

Jaya was invited to Britain in 1984 to develop a project whilst teaching ethnic minority groups and involving host communities. The project's success led to her accepting a job at the Bhartiya Vidya Bhavan in London. Her career thrived in a positive and fulfilling work place and with the support of her husband and two beautiful daughters.

Jaya's need to create nurturing dance arenas was to see the creation of a sister organisation, Abhinaya Darpan Dance Company in Glasgow in 1989. Jaya and her company have tirelessly organised charity shows and workshops to contribute to social causes locally and internationally.

Jaya's personal aims are to create opportunity and find a platform for young dedicated and committed students to expand their activities and become professionals in India's rich and ancient cultural art heritage, to encourage the development of individual skill and creativity through participation in cultural (dance, drama, music, mime and visual art), social and educational activities and to bring this awareness to the community.

# Lucky Dhillion

Lucky Dhillion. a compassionate and vibrant lady, started to work with the community as a Transport Co-ordinator with a Local Authority. helping the Asian elderly to get out and about. It was at this time that she got her first break in radio. A producer at Sina radio heard her do a voice-over for an advertisement for the transport service and asked her if she was interested in doing a Punjabi programme.

Avtar Lit, her boss at Sina radio. offered her an afternoon slot when he started Sunrise Radio. She held complete control over the content and format of her programmes, which were broadcast throughout the UK, Europe and Mauritius. Her chat show in the afternoon was very popular with wife's and mothers. She developed her own style of broadcasting.

She too was experiencing hard times as a single mother and identified with the women suffering pain, loneliness and fear. Her callers found her a warm and emphatic listener who understood their plight. Lucky is aware that after years of suffering abuse and having tried hard to make their marriage work, women need counselling and support to become more confident and self reliant. These callers helped her through her difficult times and she became much stronger as a person.

Also a talented singer, Lucky has recorded a new album. She has also been involved in a short Punjabi film about a woman who comes to stay with her estranged family in the UK and finds herself in the role of a live-in nanny.

# Anuja Dhir

Middle of three daughters Anuja Dhir was born in Dundee, Scotland in 1968. Entering university in 1984 at the age of 16, she qualified in both English and Scottish law.

Between 1986 and 1988 Anuja was the assistant editor of SCOLAG, in which her own work was also published in 1987.

In 1989 she became a member of Grays Inn, attaining the Grays Inn entrance training award, and two years later she joined the chambers of John Matthew QC in Temple.

Her professional practice consists of mainly white collar crime, judicial review and trading standards work.

Anuja Dhir

A keen sports fanatic, Anuja also enjoys public speaking and reading.

# Maria Fernandes

Maria Fernandes was born in Kenya in 1959.

Arriving in Britain at the age of 14, she went on to read law at Cardiff University. Maria qualified as a barrister in 1982 and was called to the Bar as a member of Middle Temple. She later switched to become a solicitor in 1991.

She was the secretary of the International Bar Association's Migration and Nationality Law Committee until 1994, when she became an executive member of the Law Society's Sub Committee on Immigration and was appointed to its Equal Opportunities Committee. She has recently been appointed to the Ethnic Minorities

Maria Fernandes

Advisory Committee (EMAC), which advises the Judicial Studies Board on ethnic minority issues and particularly training issues affecting the judiciary. Maria joined the city practice of

Speechly Bircham in 1989 to establish their Immigration Unit. She founded Fernandes Vaz solicitors in 1995, which specialises in immigration and nationality law and women's rights.

Maria has found that over the years, immigration law has become more complicated, particularly since the Asylum and Immigration Act 1993. In a bid to provide practical information on how to work through the appropriate forms, documents and procedures, Maria wrote the book, 'A Guide to Visitor's Visas'. She contributed a chapter 'Law Reform for All', a major survey of the Labour Party's legal thinking, and has also contributed a chapter to the 'International Taxation of Employment Manual', published by FT Law and Tax.

Maria is also currently President of the Mental Health Review Tribunal and a member of the Data Protection Tribunal.

# Baroness Shreela Flather

Active in the Conservative Party since the early 1970s, Baroness Shreela Flather has served on numerous public bodies. In 1976, she became the first ethnic minority woman councillor in Britain and, in 1986, Britain's first woman Mayor for the Royal Borough of Windsor and Maidenhead.

She has campaigned tirelessly to improve race relations and, since entering the House of Lords as a Conservative life peer in 1990, she has been able to strengthen Clause 95 of the Criminal Justice Act 1991 by making it a duty for everyone involved in the criminal justice system to avoid discriminating on racial grounds.

Baroness Shreela Flather

# Brij Lata Gandhi

Brij Lata Gandhi was born in 1939, educated and worked as a teacher in Mombasa, Kenya. A professional counsellor, Brij has acquired a very broad range of helping skills through her career.

Educated to Diploma level in Counselling and Professional Counselling, she also studied for a certificate in Marriage Guidance Counselling.

Brij began her community work in 1982 as Secretary at Sharing of Faiths Group and continued in this post until 1994. As School Board Member and Vice Chair for seven years for Hindu Mandhir, Brij initiated Religious Education, Hindiusm and Hindi 'O' level grades in school, organised religious festivals, trained young members of the community for concerts and has been the in-house marriage officer since 1986.

Until 1994, she was also Director for Needleworks, a community project which initiated community banners made

Brij Lata Gandhi

by women and put together art and craft exhibitions for the
Museum of Religion in Glasgow.

Brij was the key person in setting up Gryffe Asian Women's
Refuge and was the Director/Chair of Sahara, a youth hostel for
young black girls. Currently she is Director and Chairperson for
Meridian - Centre for Black & Ethnic Minority Women, which
she manages and supervises. The recruitment and training of
women are her priority.

With race and youth also high on Brij's social agenda, she
was a member of the Race Advisory Group and at present is a
member of Race Equality Unity of City Council in Glasgow.

Appointed Senior Project Counsellor at Youth Counselling
Services Agency in 1994, she continues to assess needs, design
and manage care plans, enhance and encourage independence
through self respect, attend to physical and spiritual needs and
deliver quality training and counselling.

# Sonia Gandhi

A black woman and a Hindu, Sonia Gandhi questions whether
she fits into any ethnic grouping or definition. A fundamental
problem with essentially white organisations and institutions
who 'lump' her with all black women in one homogeneous
mass. She refuses to be pigeon-holed into any one group,
neither will she define others to give the white organisations "a
feel good factor".

Sonia Gandhi

Born and brought up in Britain, along with most of her
generation, she feels she has the right to challenge all service
providers.

A Treasurer at Rainbow, a national forum for black and
minority women, her work to date has been towards
strengthening the resolve of women of all races, not merely
empowering them but instilling in them a sense of pride,
restoring their self-esteem and to make them realise they are
something of value.

Working in the Anti-Racism field with SCARJ (Scottish
Churches Agency for Racial Justice), she hopes to raise
awareness of the continual and accumulative racial harassment
suffered, and helps others to identify forms of prevention. For
Sonia, campaigning for racial equality is an endless round of
workshops, seminars, conferences, talks, questionnaires and
supporting local forums as well as political activities.

She also campaigns for black-led organisations and groups -
not for segregation but, very simply, to emphasise that if one of
them makes a mistake, it will be an error of judgement and not
because they are black.

Involved in investigating the effects of, and campaigning
against, the draconian Immigration and Asylum Act 1996 with

the National Black Alliance, she contributes to the research and planning of youth poverty forums throughout Glasgow.

A management committee member of Wester Hailes Against Racism Project, Sonia is also an observer on the committee for West of Scotland CRC 9Community Relation Council).

And last, but by no means least, she is simply Sonia Gandhi, wife.

# Hema Ghadiali

Hema Ghadiali, who from a very early age had an ambition to be a doctor for people with mental health problems, was born in Ahmedabad, India in 1947. Through determination and perseverance, she qualified as a psychiatrist in Gujarat and marriage to a fellow psychiatrist followed shortly afterwards.

On arriving in Britain in 1974, Hema qualified in psychiatry again and managed to get a Consultant Psychiatrist job in 1981. During this period she had three children and, because her husband's job was at different locations for five years, Hema had to manage a career, children and two houses.

In 1985, Hema became a member of Residential Care Review (A Positive Choice) set up by Norman Fawler the Minister for Social Services. An opportunity arose in 1987 for both Hema and her husband to work together as Consultant Psychiatrists in Derby, making Hema the only female ethnic minority Consultant Psychiatrist in Derby City.

Appointed as Mental Health Act Commissioner in 1988, she was also given the opportunity to act as Second Opinion Appointed Doctor for four years.

Hema has held many appointments including: executive committee member of various national organisations such as the Royal College of Psychiatrists, Transcultural Psychiatric Society and a member of the Professional Afro-Asian Women's Organisation; Chairman of the Medical Audit Committee; Medical Advisor to MIND; Secretary for Women Doctors' Forum, Overseas Doctors Association; Secretary for the British Medical Association (Derby Division).

For her it has been she says "Since I have given up attempting to be a superwoman", feel less guilty and have helped many other women to do the same.

To balance her hectic life, Hema practices Tai-chi and stress management.

# Chandra Ghosh

Chandra Ghosh was born in 1944 in Calcutta to a renowned scientist father and a mother who was head of department of

Bengali at a ladies college in Calcutta. As her parents were forward looking academics who encouraged her involvement in radical politics, Chandra continued to study until she completed her university qualifications in Calcutta, graduating from Nil Ratan Sircar Medical College I in 1967.

After completing her diploma in psychological medicine from the Conjoint Institute in Calcutta, she arrived in Britain in 1971 to complete her post graduate training and qualifications.

Accepting her first Consultant Psychiatrist post at Ashworth Special Hospital in 1977, she later moved to Broadmoor Special Hospital, where she continues to work as a Consultant Forensic Psychiatrist.

Chandra Ghosh

She has been involved with a number of women's organisations to champion the cause of female mentally abnormal offenders and is also interested in developing an appropriate service for mentally ill patients from black and ethnic minority communities.

Married to Norman Alexander Hindson, a man who shares her political beliefs, they are both actively involved in developing the mental health services for the offender patient, particularly women, both in this country and West Bengal, and hope to return to India West Bengal on retirement to be involved in developing the mental health services with other sympathetic colleagues, for which great support has been received from the State Government.

Sharing her family's enthusiasm for archaeology and ancient history, she also enjoys Rabindra Sangeet, as well as reading and listening to classical Indian music.

# Sadhana Ghose

Sadhana Ghose, Freelance Journalist, Communications Consultant and Lecturer, started her career as an investigative reporter for Thames Television's current affairs programme TV Eye and BBC's Forty Minutes series. She also contributed as an investigative reporter for Newlife Publications, Hansib Publications, Asian Times, African Times, Caribbean Times and Third World Impact.

She developed and contributed to the women's section of Videostyle magazine and also wrote the Agony Aunty column as well as editing and contributing to Shakti, a progressive political publication on matters concerning race and gender, and developing, compiling and editing the Black Media Worker's Association Bulletin.

After moving from the Bucks Examiner Newspaper as a Senior Reporter, she took up the post of Specialist Reporter in Community Affairs with Ealing Gazette in 1980. Having gained sufficient experience, she chose to freelance, research and write for various local newspapers and current affairs programme in 1982 and continued until 1992. In 1993, she was appointed London Bureau Chief of the International Observer which covered news on issues regarding the United Nations.

As well as teaching and lecturing on various development, skills, film and television courses from 1982 until 1990, Sadhana was seconded to the Kensington and Chelsea College's marketing and publicity department in 1991, when, in addition to handling the college's marketing and publicity, she organised courses for staff development on how to use the media in publicising Further Education and Adult Education courses as well as on reaching ethnic minority communities.

She assisted vice-principal Ursula Howard in 1992, in writing the Section 11 bid which was successful in obtaining funds for 3 years and is now seconded to co-ordinate the Section 11 programme in college and in addition she is teaching the Northern Examination and Assessment Board's University Entrance Trust in English Speakers of Other Languages and also developing a Home Tutoring Scheme in parent and children learning together with the aid of broadcasting.

Sadhana is currently the Co-ordinator for Community Languages with Kensington and Chelsea College of Further and Continuing Education, where her main responsibility is to research and develop courses after identifying training needs of bilinguals in the Borough, a group which also includes a large number of refugees.

She has developed and teaches Bilingual Skill Certificate courses which were validated by London's Institute of Linguists for the Bengali and Moroccan communities in the area. As well as teaching English for Speakers of Other Languages and English for Specific Purposes, she has developed Northern Examinations and Assessment Board's University Entrance Test in English for Speakers of Other Languages for the college she also teaches on this course.

# Zerbanoo Gifford

Zerbanoo Gifford was born in 1950 in India. She was educated as a child in England and went on to study at the London School of Journalism and attained a BA (Hons) degree through the Open University.

Zerbanoo began her political career in the early 1980s as a councillor for the London Borough of Harrow. In 1985 for one year she was Chair for the Commission into Ethnic Involvement in British Life. In the same year she became Chair to the Liberal Party's Community Relations Panel, a position which she held for three years. In 1987 Zerbanoo was a parliamentary candidate for Harrow East and in 1983 and 1992 for Hertsmere. In 1991 and 1993 she was elected as a member of the Liberal Democrat Federal Executive.

Zerbanoo is a Personal Advisor to the leader of the Liberal Democrats, the President of Hertsmere constituency party and a columnist for the ëLiberal Democrat News'.

Zerbanoo Gifford

Zerbanoo is the author of a number of published works including 'The Golden Thread', 'Dadabhai Naoroji'- on the centenary of the election of Britain's first Indian MP - and 'Asian Presence in Europe' which highlights the important achievements of Asians who have made a significant contribution to European society.

She was the launch editor of Libas International women's magazine, for which she was the runner-up for the Special Interest British Magazine Editor of the Year.

Zerbanoo has freelanced for a cross-section of national and international newspapers and magazines. She appears regularly on BBC's Question Time, Newsnight and Channel Four News, and Radio 4's Today, Any Questions and Woman's Hour. She is often consulted on women's, moral and inter-community issues.

Much of Zerbanoo's time is involved with charity work. She is the Director of Anti-Slavery International, the world's oldest human rights organisation, campaigning on behalf of the 200 million people still held in conditions of slavery today, an advisor to the Prince's Youth Business Trust, a council member of the Voluntary Arts Network, a Friend of the Daycare Trust campaigning for quality child-care, an advisory board member of Public Concern at Work working for morality in business, a patron of Asian Friends of the RSPCA and an executive member of the Fawcett Society. She is also a Patron of UN Year of Peace, Co-chair of D Naoroji Parliamentary Centenary and a former London Organiser for Shelter and fund-raiser for Oxfam.

Zerbanoo's work has been rewarded with the "Freedom of the City of Lincoln, Nebraska" in 1987 whilst a guest of the US government in their leadership programme. She also won The Nehru Centenary Award in 1989 for international political work, championing the cause of women and was nominated for Women of Europe Award in 1991. In 1992 she became a Fellow of the Royal Society of Arts.

She has recently completed her latest book "Thomas Clarkson and the Campaign Against Slavery", "The Golden Thread" - asian experience of Post Raj Britain. She is currently the director of The Asha Foundation.

# Gurbans K. Gill

Born in Sangrur, India in 1937, Gurbans K. Gill's roles as a successful businesswoman and a Justice of the Peace are just a tip of the iceberg in a career that has been both dynamic and ground-breaking.

Gurbans K. Gill

The eldest daughter of a Major, Gurbans attained an MA degree in Economics and a B. Ed from Punjab University. It wasn't long before she joined her husband in the Economics & Statistical Organisation in the Planning Department in the Punjab Government in Chandigarh.

Gurbans arrived in Britain in 1966 with her husband and two daughters. Her first position was at the Inland Revenue Department where she remained for five years. Deciding to use her entrepreneurial skills she then branched out on her own as a property developer and today owns three High Street Shops and two guest houses. Being a woman with a social and political conscience combined with her determined and courageous attitude to life, Gurbans became a Justice of the Peace in 1979, even though her husband had passed away not long before.

1983 saw her coming into the political and historical arena when she became District Councillor for the Social Democratic Party (1983-1991) and first Asian women County Councillor of Buckinghamshire (1983-1993) again for the SDP. Her victory was particularly significant because it was a strong Conservative constituency with very few Asian residents.

As politics and social awareness go hand in hand so did Gurbans career path. In 1983 she became the Chairperson of the School Governing Body till 1993, a member of the Thames Valley Police Authority (1985-1993) and a member of their Complaints Committee. In 1990 she acquired title 'Lady of the Manor of Stapleton'. Then in 1991 she was elected Vice chairperson of the Police Consultative Committee till 1993. Not content with her achievements and her positive actions she served on the Buckinghamshire County Council, Social Services, Personnel, Trading Standards, Child Abuse and Land & Property Committees. A woman striving for a better social environment she is also running her own campaign against Drug & Alcohol Abuse.

Amazingly Gurbans has also squeezed in the time to write and publish two of her own poetry books.

## Indpreet Kaur Goel

Telling her parents as a child that she wanted to become an engineer to help her civil engineer father repair his cars, Indpreet Goel is the first Asian woman to achieve Technical Management Grade in British Airways.

Born in Dar es Salaam, Tanzania in 1969, Indpreet's early education was at the International School of Tanganyika, where she completed her O levels, and divulged in her passions of acting and swimming for which she won all the medals and awards the school could offer by the age of 10. Arriving in the UK in 1985, she went to the Royal Masonic School for Girls in Rickmansworth to complete her A levels. Moving on to the University of Southampton to graduate as a B.Eng Hons in Electronic Engineering, she completed her MSc, specialising in Artificial Intelligence at the Queen Mary and Westfield College of London University.

Joining the British Airways engineering department in 1992, her achievements include the introduction of cabin defects coding and the use of ACARS - Airborne Communication Addressing and Reporting System.

Indpreet Kaur Goel

She is an associate member of Neighbourhood Engineers, a section of the Engineering Council, through which she attends schools to promote engineering and encourage girls to embark on a career formerly not acceptable for females.

She is currently working in Supply Chain developing Man Management Skills at British Airways and confesses she is doing exactly what she dreamed of as a child, except that, instead of rebuilding cars, she is rebuilding flight systems, with the bonus of indulging in her favourite hobby of travelling the world. Any spare time is spent listening to Hindi classical and English music, as well as playing the guitar, tampura, harmonium, keyboard and santoor.

# Sukhneel Kaur Goel

A specialist in family law, Sukhneel Goel is also actively involved in law–related community work.

Born in Dar es Salaam, Tanzania in 1967, Sukhneel was sent to the private International School of Tanganyika. Participating in many activities, Sukhneel won numerous awards in many activities including ASA (honours level) in swimming, First Aid, Duke of Edinburgh champion in Chess, Leader Debating Team and an all round best student.

Arriving in England in 1982, Sukhneel studied up to A level at the Rickmansworth Masonic School for Girls. Encouraged to pursue a legal career, she read Law at the University of Reading, graduating as LLB (Hons), and the Law Society College in Guildford.

Sukhneel Kaur Goel

Joining Mackenzie Prasaud in 1990 as an article clerk, she quickly realised she wanted to specialise in family law.

As secretary, fund raiser and legal adviser at Southall Rights and on the panel of the Society of Asian Lawyers, she regularly provides free advice on legal matters.

Regularly attending meetings organised by local groups in Harrow, she is kept up to date with grass roots work on issues relating to women, child welfare and counselling. Now a partner is St. Johns Solicitors, Sukhneel is well on the way to achieving the goals she set out for herself when she began her legal career.

# Azmina Govindji

Azmina Govindji

A qualified nutritionist who has specialised in Asian diets and health, Azmina Govindji has spent eight years as Chief Dietitian to the British Diabetic Association. Now a freelance consultant and food writer, she frequently appears on BBC, Sky and Cable TV as well as radio.

Author of several cookbooks, including "Quick and Easy Curries" for Sainsbury's and "Feast From the East" a calorie counted Asian cookbook for Weight Watchers, she is currently working on her 6th book and planning a series of radio programmes on Asian food and health which will be broadcast throughout the UK.

Born in Uganda and brought up in Edinburgh, Scotland, Azmina identified well with the Scottish community and never felt 'different' to be Asian. Her knowledge of Gujarati became an asset when learning the pronunciation of European languages. Taking mainly science subjects at school, Azmina went on to study nutrition at the University of London in 1976, qualifying as a State Registered Dietitian in 1981.

After practising as a therapeutic dietician in several London hospitals, Azmina's first big career break came in 1987 when she became Chief Dietician and Head of Diet Information Services at the British Diabetic Association. She acted as the national consultant on diet and diabetes for doctors, nurses and other health professionals as well as people with diabetes. She wrote articles for magazines and professional journals and produced consumer education materials which are used by hospitals and GP surgeries throughout the country. Azmina represented the British Diabetic Association in influencing food labelling and legislation of manufactured foods.

Azmina's personal interest in the Asian diet led her to set up the Ethnic Group Advisory Panel of the British Diabetic Association – a multi-disciplinary team responsible for improving the care of Asian people with diabetes. She produced translated leaflets for Asian people and delivered presentations to doctors, dietitians and other professionals on the specific dietary and cultural practices of the Asian community in Britain.

Her second, even bigger break (little known to her at the time) came in 1995 after having two children, she decided the position demanded too much of her time whilst looking after a home and young family. Leaving work in 1995, Azmina started her own part-time consultancy as a freelance Nutritionist and Dietitian. Never looking back, she feels she is getting the best of both worlds – a stimulating career balanced with a commitment to her family.

Strongly believing that if you give to others you will be giving more to yourself, she has been involved in voluntary work within her community since the age of 14.

# Charanjit Kaur Grover

Charanjit Kaur Grover, daughter of Sardar Bahadur Santokh Singh Sodhi, was born into an affluent family in Calcutta. Charanjit is now a Justice of the Peace for the The Middlesex Commission Area in Britain.

Charanjit Kaur Grover

After early schooling in Darjeeling, India, encouraged by her parents to achieve academically, Charanjit enrolled at Miranda College, Delhi University for her BA degree. Just 6 months away from completing her degree, she met her husband to be. After graduation, Charanjit was married in 1966 and arrived in Britain a few days later.

Having her own nanny as a child and never being exposed to the day-to-day running of a home, Britain was a culture shock for Charanjit. Feeling isolated except for the company of an old English neighbour, Charanjit would keep herself busy with daily chores around the house. Her main company was her husband who was running a successful and flourishing business, and her two brothers-in-law. It wasn't until almost two years later, when Charanjit met the elder sister of an old school friend, that she had the company of another Asian female.

With encouragement from her husband, Charanjit built up the confidence to work, applying for a post with Midland Bank in their Head Office Audit Department. Being a BA graduate and having done book-keeping and accounts, she was hired immediately upgraded to a high salary. Thoroughly enjoying her work, Charanjit began to settle down and feel at home in Britain. An executive officer by the time her son was born, Charanjit decided to spend more time with her family. With the birth of their daughter, Charanjit continued in her role as full-time mother.

Once the children were old enough to attend nursery, Charanjit began to help her husband with their property Development Business and decided to work independently when her daughter was at senior school.

Charanjit was selected to be a Magistrate by the Lord Chancellor's Department and, during the selection interview, she was given an opportunity to put her own questions to the panel. Among these was confirmation of how she was expected to dress while sitting in the court as a Magistrate. She had attended the interview wearing a salwar, khameez, dupatta and shawl and the panel unanimously agreed that her National Dress was the most suitable.

As a Magistrate for the Adult Court and Youth Court, she feels privileged for the opportunity to be representative of the Asian community within the British Legal System.

In addition to her role as Justice of the Peace, Charanjit is a Health Adviser, in which capacity she has produced information documents for first generation Asians. She has also organised workshops and given talks in seminars arranged by the Department of Health. Charanjit finds doing community work provides stimulation and allows her to give something back into the community.

# Indu Gupta

Indu Gupta

Dr Indu Gupta, was born in Maharashtra, India in 1939. Her father was involved in the settlement of refugees in Chembur, Kalyan and Pimpri (Poona) camps which caused disruption in her school life but enabled her to learn Marathi, Gujarati, English, Hindi and Punjabi.

In 1961 Indu graduated in Medicine and shortly after marrying Dr SC Gupta, they arrived in Britain in 1965. With support from her husband, Indu attained a diploma and went on to qualify with MRC and FRCs in Pathology. She was appointed a Consultant in Histopathology at the Wigan and Leigh group of hospitals under the North West Regional Authority in 1979.

Indu is Chair of the regional Clinical Audit Committee, has published academic papers and lectured to various local medical groups.

Joining the Soroptimist International of Wigan in 1984, she was the president of the club during 1990 - 1991 and organised a competition to mark the Golden Jubilee of the Club. She participates in the charity and service work of the club, which includes lecturing to various women's groups on Hinduism and Eastern culture, and promoting East West relations at a local level.

However, Indu feels her greatest commitment to her two children, a daughter who graduated with an MSc from Guy's Hospital and is now a dentist and her son, who is working at the National Institute of Medical Research for his PhD in Genetics.

# Rahila Gupta

Rahila Gupta

Rahila Gupta, a writer, journalist and political activist, whose "work in Britain has in some way, been involved with the struggle against injustice", was born in London in 1956.

On completing her BA in English Literature and French at Bombay University, Rahila returned to England in 1975. She continued her education at the University of Westminster, obtaining a M. Phil in English Drama.

She has been active in anti-racist, feminist and disability equality campaigns and has edited "Shakti" – a bi-monthly magazine for Asian youth. She was also a member of the editorial collective of "Outwrite"– a monthly feminist, anti-imperialist and anti-racist newspaper.

Rahila has worked as a freelance journalist for a variety of newspapers and magazines in Britain, India and Sri Lanka. She has published short stories and poetry and co-edited two collections of short stories from the Asian Women Writers Collective, of which she is a founder member.

Rahila is presently ghosting the autobiography of Kiranjit Ahluwalia "Circle of Light", to be published in 1997. She is a member of the management collective of Southhall Black Sisters.

# Nazim Hamid

Nazim Hamid, for whom experiences as a first generation Asian going through the education system, was at times "very painful and isolating", is an Administrator and Finance Officer for the Glasgow Council for Single Homeless.

Born in Britain in 1966, the family moved to Scotland in the early 1980s. During her educational years, she felt there was very little support and no real frame of reference for girls from minority families. The most difficult element was the conflict of identity for children who felt they were Asian, British or both. At that time, as today, these pressures were not really recognised and for Nazim this was a difficult period in her life. She left school with a solid list of "O" levels and Highers in Biology, English and Chemistry.

Nazim Hamid

Nazim's social awareness and concern for women, ethnic minorities and society at large naturally led her to community work. Her training has included: Advocacy in Discrimination at Commission for Racial Equality London: Discrimination & Race Relation Act at Glasgow University; Counselling for Childline; HIV and AIDS at Childline and Network respectively.

Today, Nazim feels that she has progressed without compromising her identity as an Asian woman. Training schemes are an essential part for people leaving the education system. Her main concern is for Asian women who have the added handicap of language, culture, social stereotyping and the lack of recognition given for the strength, skills and experiences which could benefit society as a whole.

Through her work with the community, Nazim has had several personal achievements. She was a member of two Steering Commitees; a Campaign for Justice - dealing with discrimination in the judicial system; and Rainbow - promoting the identity and needs of black and ethnic minority women in Scotland. She is also on the Management Committee for the Govanhill Youth Project, which strives to meet the needs of young people from different minorities in Govanhill.

She feels her greatest achievement, however, comes from being an Asian woman, feeling enriched her through culture and community. She states, " being Asian gives my life an added value and I am more of a person for this".

With her adventurous spirit and insight into life, Nazim reads, gets involved in community activities, enjoys cinema and the arts and tries her hand at all kind of sport, including golf.

# Ayesha Hasan

Ayesha Hasan

Ayesha Hasan was born in London of Pakistani parent and is the third generation and the first female in her family to become a Barrister. She grew up in Nigeria, where her father was appointed a judge, later rising to become Chief Justice of Sokoto State in Nigeria. Her mother was the first female in her family to go overseas from Lahore in search of higher education. Both of Ayesha's parents were very keen that their daughter pursue a career of her choice.

By the age of 10, Ayesha already knew she wanted to study law. She attended Ahmadu Bello University in Zaria, where she had her first real exposure to jurisprudence and what was later to become her specialist area of practice, an introduction to Islamic Law. She topped her year and was awarded an LLB (Hons) degree in July 1984 as well as receiving prizes for jurisprudence and for being the best overall student of the year.

She went on to do her Masters in law from Queen's College, Cambridge in 1985 and enrolled at the Honourable Society of Gray's Inn, like her father and grandfather before her, and was called to the Bar in July 1987. She became at tenant at 3 Dr Johnson's Buildings, Temple in 1989 where she practised general common law. She later specialised in family law and has now got a healthy family law practice with the special ability of being able to assist Asian and Muslim families in cases which involve Islamic family laws.

As well as being the first ethnic member to join chambers, Ayesha has since broken other boundaries. She was elected on to the Committee of the Family Law Barristers Association and became the first Asian to do so. She is on the committee of the Commonwealth Ethnic Barristers Association and a member of the London Legal Aid Area Committee.

Besides law, which is certainly her passion, Ayesha's other interests include travelling. Amongst some of the places she has visited have been China, where she climbed the Great Wall. She has watched the sunset over the Grand Canyon, stood in awe at the power of the waterfalls of Niagara and taken in the beauty and majesty of the Taj Mahal. In 1994, she joined a total of two million pilgrims to perform what was to be an unforgettable experience, the Haj.

Despite having undertaken all this, Ayesha still feels that she has a lot more ground to cover, both professionally and geographically.

# Roshan Horabin

Roshan Horabin was born into a wealthy merchant family in India in 1924 and was educated at Cathedral and John Canon High School, Bombay. In 1945 she married Ivan Horabin, a British naval officer, son of a Liberal Chief Whip.

Roshan Horabin

As a young girl aged eight, Roshan made her first of many visits to prisons and slums, helping her mother with her work as a social worker concerning health and literacy in Bombay. This early exposure to isolation and deprivation led her to a lifetime's concern with social conditions and shaped her life's work. Further experience was gained when in 1939, she joined the St. John's Ambulance Society under the auspices of Lady Mountbatten. She and Hon Bina Sinha were the only Indians to be assigned to work in the European section of the Prisoner Of War Intelligence Department, compiling reports on and interviewing prisoners.

In 1946, the year following her marriage, Roshan arrived in war-ravaged Liverpool to set up home. Residing mainly in London because her husband's parents lived close to Westminster, she raised their three daughters, whilst studying for a sociology degree. An active member of the Girl Guide Council at Guide Headquarters and with Brownies in Westminster. She was also the first ethnic appointee to the Board of Governors of Greycoat Hospital School and Queen Anne's, Caversham. She joined the prestigious Howard League for Penal Reform and the Institute for the Study and Treatment of Delinquents, to whose Council of Management she was subsequently appointed. In 1958 she was invited by the Blackfriars Settlement to befriend prisoners and visit prisons, and two years later became the first ethnic member of The New Bridge - a charity for befriending prisoners. She still visits Asian prisoners and their families today.

In 1967, when her youngest daughter went on to university, she scored another significant first when she was appointed as an ethnic Probation Officer in Britain and was subsequently awarded the Home Office Diploma.

Her zeal for penal reform led to several radio and television discussions on the subject. In 1976 she was awarded a Cropwood Fellowship from the Institute of Criminology, Cambridge. The first Asian to be allowed into prisons for research, she published *Problems of Asians in Penal Institutions* in 1978. As a result of this, she was invited by the Home Office to lecture to Prisons Governors and other related groups. Following her recommendations, race relations officers were appointed in prisons and information packs were made available to prisoners. She is much in demand as an authoritative speaker on India and the Raj and was a visiting professor taking seminars on E. M. Forster's A Passage to India in the USA.

Roshan took early retirement from the Probation Service in 1986 but continues her research and campaigning and is a voluntary counsellor for victims of crime, rape and bereavement in the county where she lives. A founder member of India Women's Association started by Vijaylakshmi Pandit, she stills remains very much the backbone of the association. She was also present in London when the All Pakistan Women's Association was formed, and continues to support both Asian women's charities in their work for the community.

# Foqia Hayee

Foqia Hayee

Foqia Hayee has been a councillor for Lewisham since May 1994 representing the Churchdown Ward in the Downham area of the Borough and is Lewisham's first Asian woman Mayor.

She is a graphic designer by education and an experienced primary school teacher.

Before being elected as a Councillor, she represented Older Women's projects on behalf of the Council abroad and helped form the Older Women's Network.

She was the first woman to be elected Chair of the Pensioners' Committee, following her election as a Councillor. Serving on various committees including Women's, Community Affairs, Housing, Social Services and the CHC (Community Health Council), as well as being Chair of the People with Learning Difficulties Committee, she is currently on the democracy project, involved in the Millennium working party and the quality commission provision for the elderly.

As Mayor she is now an ex-officio member of all Council Committees and takes a keen interest in the Early Years sub-committee as well as being a school governor.

Her special interests include finding ways to develop and maintain links between the young and old as well as concerns about playgrounds for the young people of Lewisham, which she believes should use the most up-to-date equipment to provide physical and mental stimulation. Being an Asian she will aid any events to support awareness in the community, especially among women and children, and will encourage all ethnic minorities to take an active part in local politics with the provision of permanent meeting places for ethnic minority groups.

She has been successful in initiating an Orienteering Project in her local Beckenham Place Park and is starting a pilot project to create links between the older and younger generations.

# Shahrukh Husain

Born in Karachi in 1950, Pakistan, Shahrukh Husain experienced a profoundly synthesised blend of cultural elements as she grew up to the sounds of women's voices organising the country, giving her the feeling that women ran the world though they often stepped aside to give men the credit.

Involved in organising her aunt's campaign to the national assembly in 1970, she ran a leading monthly magazine, Women's World, of which she became editor prior to arriving in London at the age of 21.

Her first six months in London were spent working for The Competitors Journal before going on to freelance, including providing publicity for film and television companies.

Taking a break to continue her education, Shahrukh graduated with an honours degree in South Asian Studies with Arabic from School of Oriental and African Studies in 1979, then an M. Phil in Modern Urdu Poetry which was upgraded to a PhD in 1980.

Returning to the world of publishing, Shahrukh began work with the Middle East Economic Digest (MEED). She married Prof. Christopher Shacle. Still working at MEED as an Associate Editor, she gave birth to her son in 1982. After becoming a Consultant, she produced three bilingual directories of the Middle East, one of which won the Queen's Jubilee Award.

A good place to develop her passion for films, Shahrukh joined the British Board of Film Classification as a Senior Examiner, as well as teaching Urdu and culture to foreign office diplomats prior to their departure for Pakistan.

Using her knowledge of writing, broadcasting and teaching, she wrote the script in collaboration with Anita Desai for her screenplay adaptation of her novel In Custody and in 1994 it was nominated for Oscar for Best Film in a Foreign Language. She has also translated and co-edited a number of BBC documentaries, including Ashes and Dust.

As well as writing Focus on India and Exploring Indian Food, Shahrukh edited Floella Benjamin's book on West Indian food in the same series. Researching and writing A Megawicked Story and Mecca, she edited and introduced Virago Book of Witches which is one of Virago's greater successes in hardback.

Rolling all her experiences into one, she has given several seminars on subjects relating to Indian cinema, Indo-Anglian women writers and the experience of immigration and displacement, whilst continuing to contribute to anthologies and encyclopaedias on folklore, film and Urdu poetry.

Shahrukh was commissioned by Newham Drug Prevention Through Puppet Theatre to write an anti-drugs play, an Inter Cultural therapist with Jungian Bias she currently works as a psychotherapist.

# Shehzad Husain

Shehzad Husain

Shehzad Husain is a cookery expert who can be said to be the pivotal person behind Marks & Spencer's astoundingly successful range of Indian foods. In addition to being their cookery consultant, she is also advisor to British Airways and is often consulted by various food manufacturers on Asian cuisine.

Belonging to a distinguished Deccan Hyderabadi family, Shehzad was born in Karachi and since her school days in the early 60's has lived in London. She owes much of her inspiration to her mother, emulating her Hyderabadi culinary delicacies and at the same time adding her own touch through exploration and experimentation.

With a passion that went beyond a hobby, Shehzad soon discovered the endless diversity of the culinary culture of the Indo-Pakistani sub-continent. She taught cookery at the Orpington Adult Education Centre between 1983 and 1985 and gave cookery lessons and demonstrations at the Cordon Bleu School in London.

A prolific writer of books on the cuisines of India and Pakistan, her publications include the successful Entertaining Indian Style which sold 30,000 copies; An Indian Table ; Low Fat Indian Cookery; The Balti Cook Book; Vegetarian Indian Cookery; Shehzad Husain's Easy Indian Cookery and Healthy Indian Cooking. She has co-authored The Complete Book of Indian Cooking and has contributed feature articles on cookery in periodicals such as Family Circle; Woman; Libas; and Food Aid.

Shehzad has demonstrated her expertise on national television programmes, such as Kilroy; Daytime Live; and Pebble Mill; and has had regular slots on TV Asia. In addition, she has appeared on various radio shows on BBC World Service, Radio 4 and various commercial stations.

Shehzad is married with three children.

# Meena Jafarey

Meena Jafarey

Born in London, Meena Jafarey is a visual artist and works for the charity Artsline.

After leaving school, she took time out and travelled to Pakistan, India and Thailand. Soon after her return to Britain, Meena was involved in a serious road accident which left her disabled. During her convalescence, she began painting and then decided to go to Art College to study fine art. After completing her degree, she found herself a studio and continues to work there. She has had regular exhibitions of her work in this country and abroad and became involved in community arts, working on a number of art projects with the local community.

In her work with Artsline, London's information and advice

service on the arts and entertainment for disabled people, as an ethnic arts officer for Multicultural Protect which provides culturally specific information to disabled people, she is committed to working towards better services and equality for disabled people from the ethnic communities.

Meena also sits on a number of committees at the Arts Council of England and has been a UK delegate at the Women's Caucus for the Arts conference in the USA. She was recently in Lahore on an International Arts workshop and will be exhibiting in New York in October 1997.

# Sharmila Jandial

Sharmila Jandial was born and brought up in Aberdeen, Scotland. She became the first Asian female President of Glasgow University's Man's Union, which between 1885 and 1980 has been an all male and independent institution.

She has served on the Board of Management since 1995 and expresses that it is a great way of meeting people and providing a sense of responsibility.

The 20 year old is following in the footsteps of her parents, who are both doctors, and is studying medicine at Glasgow University.

# Annand Jasani

Describing herself as a multi-lingual Welsh-Tanzanian-Indian with a global perspective, Annand Jasani is the daughter of Sikh parents, brought up in Tanzania and educated at Catholic and Islamic schools. Who has since settled in Britain and is married to a Hindu Gujarati-speaking doctor.

Being heavily influenced from a very young age by her brilliant playwright-cum-actor-cum-poet father, Annand has developed a longstanding, almost devotional, interest in the performing arts, especially stage acting and singing. Over her past thirty years in Britain, this has led her to play leading roles in several major Indian as well as Welsh theatre productions, including Red Oleandors and Kanchan Rang (East-West Theatre Company, Birmingham - 1973-1977), Tristan and Essellt, Twm Son Cati and Madog (Theatre Taliesin, Cardiff, 1985-1989) and Dhong and Uljan (Natak Theatre Company, Cardiff, 1990-1995).

Annand Jasani

Her stage personality and acting ability has also landed her several roles in television documentaries and series, including commentator in India Comes to Grange Town (Between Cultures, BBC Wales TV, 1988), demonstrator of her expertise in Indian Cookery (See You Sunday, BBC Wales, 1990), Social

Commentator (People, HTV, 1993), Dr Jani (Welsh Hospital soap Glan Hafren, 1994) and a cameo role (Pobol Y Cwm, HTV, 1995).

Her biggest break in the world of media came in 1987 when she was elected by BBC Radio Wales as a producer/presenter to set up an Asian Magazine programme with a global Welsh-Asian perspective. She very aptly chose to call the programme A Voice for All, which has since become a household name in Wales and the surrounding regions in England. Her dedicated industriousness and innovative approach has ensured uninterrupted, regular live broadcast of the programme over the past 10 years. Annand is an intrepid and confident presenter with an endearing style who has interviewed many local, national and international personalities, including Mother Theresa, the Dalai Lama, Sir Richard Attenborough, Vanessa Redgrave and Ravi Shankar.

Annand's contributions have been widely recognised and acknowledged. She is a member of Equity and her work has received critical acclaim from a number of critics, including Western Mail Radio Critic Gwyn Griffiths. She has received several prestigious awards including Asian DJ and Community awards from Apna Beat (1994, 1995) and Asian Film Academy (1994). She has been nominated for the Race in the Media (1997) and Focus (1997) awards in the Best Entertainment and Specialist Music Categories. Her greatest ambition is to run her own chat show with an Asian perspective on television.

Annand has often been described as a 'Super Woman' by people who know of her numerous selfless contributions to community work. During her 18 years as a full-time English and Business Studies teacher, she took the opportunity to widely promote within the school sector the awareness of Indian culture, arts, cookery and comparative religion. For being a member of the Welsh Arts Council Drama Committee (1987-1990), the Welsh National Opera's Education Committee and Women in Enterprise, Annand was nominated for Welsh Woman of the Year community award.

She is currently a Lay Visitor with the Vale of Glamorgan Police Authority, a Trustee of Cardiff and District Multicultural Arts Development (CADMAD) and the newly elected Chairperson of Golden Anniversary of Independence Celebrations Association (GAICA) in Wales.

# Shobana Jeyasingh

Born in Madras, now living in London, Shobana Jeyasingh has directed the Shobana Jeyasingh Dance Company since 1988. Her choreography for the company includes Palimpest (1996) Romance ... with footnotes (1993), Making of Maps (1992),

New Cities Ancient Lands (1991), Correspondences (1990), Defile (1989) and Configurations (1988).

Her work for television includes Duets with Automobiles (for the Arts Council/BBC Series) which was shortlisted for the IMZ Dance Screen Award Frankfurt, Map of Dreams (After Image Productions) and Dancing by Numbers (Bandung File) for Channel 4, Late for The Late Show and a Network East Dance Special for the BBC. She is currently making a documentary with the BBC to be shown Autumn 1997.

Shobana Jeyasingh

Her work for theatre includes Twelfth Night for the Theatre Royal, Stratford East and The Little Clay Cart for the Royal National Theatre. She has choreographed new work in Canada, Amsterdam and Finland as well as for The Women's Playhouse Trust, for whom she created a work for students of an East London school as part of its Life in the City series.

Shobana was awarded a London Dance and Performance award in 1988, received her third Digital Dance award in 1992 and, in 1993, an Arts Council Women in the Arts Project award to acknowledge her valuable contribution to the arts over the past decade. She has also been awarded two Time Out Dance awards and, in 1993, her company was overall winner of the Prudential Award for the Arts, one of the UK's most prestigious awards. Shobana was awarded the MBE in 1995 for services to dance and holds an honorary MA from Surrey University and honorary doctorate from De Montfort University, Leicester. She is patron of the Bristol Centre for Performing Arts, which is scheduled to open in the millennium.

# Dalia Jolly

Dalia Jolly was born in Chiswick, London in 1968 and, after early schooling and 'A' levels, went on to graduate with a BSc (Hons), MCOptom and an MSc (EHB) as well as diplomas specialising in optometrics.

Trained at Moorfields Eye Hospital, Dalia now works as a Senior Optometrist in a City of London practice.

A keen netball player, Dalia was previously a netball umpire to the City University, London and a member of the All England Netball Association and presently is a member of Islington and Deptford netball clubs.

She enjoys most sports and aerobics, as well as line dancing and is a keen cinema and theatre-goer.

# Gunita Jolly

Gunita Jolly was born in New Delhi in 1964 and came to England as a young child in 1966. Studying at Guy's Hospital,

London University for her medical degree, she qualified and worked in house jobs in Bath and London. Whilst working she was a volunteer with 'Rape Crises' organisation.

Gunita travelled alone for 3 months to Australia before commencing a 3 year GP training scheme in Greenwich. Since completion she has worked as a partner in a Blackheath General Practice, as well as taking six months out to backpack around South America and Africa.

Having sat her postgraduate exams during the last three years, Gunita has married and moved to Paris where she is involved in community work; concentrating on Asian families in Paris including the city Gurudewara. She is involved with the French Asian Women's organisation and hope to provide health care and counselling with Asian touch.

Her life revolves around medicine and travel but she takes every opportunity to read novels, history, politics and anything she can get her hands on.

Gunita Jolly

# Sujata Jolly

Sujata Jolly

Sujata Jolly, an Asian pioneer in Western cosmetology, was born and brought up in Kenya. Her memories reminiscences of childhood are of sport, fun and freedom to develop a career for herself. Moving to India in 1965 for higher education in medicine, her passion for learning through experimentation often brought her into conflict with the traditional teaching of science subjects in India, where the emphasis has remained on memorising rather than understanding. Marrying Parmod Jolly, a successful scientist, in 1968, they emigrated to the UK in the same year.

Sujata's career began in the research laboratories of ICI. Seizing all opportunities of further education to help her career, she realised her ambition to specialise in cosmetology.

1982 was a momentous year for Sujata. She left the cosy world of secure employment for the challenging life of self-employment. She started her own company 'Depeche Mode Laboratories' with the company motto of Simplitas, Probitas, Integritas.

She has scored many achievements in her work, for example developing Oxypeel, a successful treatment for a wide spectrum of skin problems which is recommended by surgeons and dermatologists, and introducing Hi-lines, the art of permanent make up. Sujata's latest innovation is Epil-pro, a system for hair removal based on static and sound energy, which some consider as the most significant development in permanent hair removal in more than seven decades.

Sujata regularly discusses skin problems on radio and television and some, is actively involved in a campaign against skin lightening products mainly used by African and Asian women.

Sujata regularly exhibits at beauty trade shows around the country

# Mahmuda Kabir

Mahmuda Kabir, whose main objective is to help deprived and needy women and children, was born in Bangladesh in 1942.

A qualified social worker since 1964, Mahmuda has a string of degrees to her name including a BA in English and Economics, an MA in Social Welfare and an MSc in Social Administration.

Since her arrival in Britain in 1966, she has also continued to pursue her passion for politics which has led her to canvass for many worthy causes.

She has held a number of posts in Public Office which include Councillor for London Borough of Lewisham, elected member from Ethnic Minority Groups of Inner London Education Authority, Joint Secretary of the Asian Forum (UK), Member of the National Regional Women's Committee and London Labour Women's Network, Secretary for the Lewisham Anti-Racist Activity Group, and most recently, as a prospective candidate for a member of Parliament.

Mahmuda's political stance has always been to the left and in support of this view she remains a member of the Labour Party. Her tireless work as an activist of the Trade Unions has also been prominent.

Mahmuda's fusion of social and political interests keeps her well aware of current social problems and various legislative changes.

# Sandhya Kapitan

Sandhya Kapitan was born and brought up in South Africa in a family that has always been actively involved in community work, charity fund-raising and the struggle for equality. She was first in her class and year throughout her high school years and the "DUX" of her high school at the age of 16, winning the "Gold Medal" for being tops as well as an all rounder. She was the first ex-scholar invited by her Alma Mater to be the Guest of Honour at an Annual Awards ceremony.

Graduating with BA and LLB degrees with distinctions after five years at university, Sandhya was the first law graduate offered a job immediately as a lecturer in Law at the university of Durban - West Ville. Lecturing to postgraduates in Roman Law, Contract Law and Interpretation of Statutes, she spent six years

Sandhya Kapitan

as an academic, covering a period both before and after working as a legal practitioner.

Moving on to serve a two year period of Articles of Clerkship, she had the Right of Appearance in Court throughout. Admitted as an Attorney of the Supreme Court of South Africa in 1977 after passing her Professional Examinations, Sandhya was the first Asian woman lawyer in her home city of Pietermaritzburg - law having been a predominantly male profession. Also passing her conveyancing examinations, she was admitted as a Conveyancer of the Supreme Court.

Sandhya has been in the UK since 1983, residing mainly in Scotland. Taking a 10 year break from her career to bring up her family, she regards this as the best investment in their lives that she has made. Having made a decision to embark on a career change, during the latter part of her stay at home, she did the MBA (Magister of Business Administration) part-time over three years. Returning to work when the children were at school, she successfully gained employment as a Business Advisor at the Ethnic Minority Enterprise Centre working with all sections of the community. Sandhya was very successful in making the mainstream agencies aware of the needs of the ethnic communities and sourced considerable sums of money for various activities involving these communities, in particular Asian women.

Currently a Business Development Manager at the Wise Group of Companies in Glasgow, her role is wide-ranging and includes, identifying and creating new business development opportunities and "socially franchising" the Wise Group 'Intermediate Labour Market' model to other parts of the UK.

With too little representation of black women in mainstream senior managerial positions, Sandhya represents an important role model who has acknowledged her self-worth and has broken through the 'glass ceiling' of inequality.

# Nadya Kassam

Born in Dar-Es-Salaam, Tanzania in 1967 and arriving in Britain in 1971, Nadya Kassam is the editor of the first anthology by young Asian women in Britain, Telling It Like It Is - Young Asian Women Talk, published by The Women's Press.

Winning the WH Smith Children's Literary Competition in 1979 was the first endorsement of her writing. She was a member of a writing workshop funded by the Inner London Education Authority and so got the opportunity to learn how to write creatively and enter the competition.

However, writing took a back seat for a while as career

choices had to be made. Her parents encouraged her to pursue science subjects, rather than arts, and so she graduated with an honors degree in Agricultural Botany from the University of Reading in 1990.

This was possibly the second non-stereotypical thing that she did, against a backdrop of Asian peers who were choosing accountancy, dentistry and medicine. The first had been to declare that she would take a 'year out' before going to university and this was spent working in British Home Stores, earning her first wage and learning to become more independent.

Nadya Kassam

On graduation, decisions had already been made that an academic career was not for her - a PhD was not going to be the course of action for her and so aspirations of working overseas as an agricultural botanist came to an end. Instead, she applied to be a volunteer for the Royal National Institute for the Blind, in their press office, hoping to gain some media experience. By luck, there was a short term position available as an assistant on a national eye safety campaign. This was the beginning of a freelance career.

Toward the middle of 1991, she decided that she wanted to travel to India and had saved up enough money for the trip. Many of her white school friends had done this after 'A' levels and she felt that it was about time she did the same. Travelling there with a companion who decided to return home after three days, Nadya continued to back-pack and after three months had been around Rajasthan, Delhi, Bombay and Goa. She ended her trip by visiting relations in Karachi and also travelled to Hunza and Gilgit in the far north of Pakistan.

On her return, she continued her work in the voluntary sector undertaking various campaigning roles around the issues of education for people with disabilities and social security benefits.

Having had the benefit of learning about disability politics, she decided to educate herself about other minority politics - women's issues, sexuality and race. As a result she became a member of the Diaspora Women's Collective, a group of 20 Black women who produced Britain's first ever Black women's newspaper on International Women's Day in March 1994.

The media experience and confidence which producing the newspaper gave her, inspired her to investigate further opportunities in film and television. To date, she has worked on a series of three documentaries for the BBC about disability charities and two short independent films, one of which was taken to the Cannes Film Festival.

In her spare time, Nadya volunteers for a fund-raising committee for her community and facilitates an Asian women's support group.

# Harbans Kaur

Harbans Kaur

Harbans Kaur was born in Gujernwala, now Pakistan, on 15th March 1913. After married Sadar Nanak Singh a Prosecuting Inspector with the police, on 7th August 1930. They had eight children – seven sons and one daughter.

Harban's husband, a local leader and the president of Shromani Gurdwara Parbandak Committee (SGPC),opposed the partition of India on religious grounds. On 5th March 1947, students of DAV College in Multan demonstrated against the imminent partition. Nanak Singh, being a local leader, went to the rescue of the students and was killed in the ensuing riots. He was honoured by the community and his picture now hangs in the Shaid gallery in the Golden Temple in Amritsar, along with other martyrs.

Widowed at the age of 34, Harbans Kaur, along with her eight children was forced to leave her native land and settled in Patiala, India. She refused to give up her children to an orphanage, and decided to cope with the tremendous responsibility of bringing them up alone. Joining the Punjab Government as a rehabilitation officer, she helped to settle the refugees who were victims of partition. She encouraged and supported her children to study hard. Five of her sons joined the defence services of India as commission officers. Two of her sons immigrated to the United Kingdom and now own successful businesses.

Harbans Kaur became a head teacher after completing her job as rehabilitation officer. Her five commission officer sons actively served for the defence of India as a result of, for this she was honoured by the Punjab Government a 'Proudest Punjabi Mother' she receives a war pension and their services for the Indian armed forces.

Harbans Kaur is an epitome of Indian women, instilling the same values in her daughter. In the face of all the odds, she rises above to do the best for her family and her county, India. She has lived in Middlesex for many years, where she relaxes in the company of two of her two sons and her many grand children.

# Permindar Kaur

Permindar Kaur, who would most like to answer the question "where is home" is a sculptor/installation artist and lecturer.

Born in Nottingham in 1965, even at school Permindar knew what her vocation in life would be and studied to gain a B.A. Hons in Fine Art from Sheffield City Polytechnic in 1989. In the same year she received an Individual Production Award from Yorkshire Arts and in 1990 she went to the prominent Glasgow School of Art, where she obtained her MA in Fine Art in 1992.

Permindar soon realised that in Britain she was expected to produce work that directly related to her being Indian, so when the opportunity arose to live and work in Barcelona she grabbed the hand of fortune. Whilst in Spain, and free from the ties of ethnicity she was able to explore a wider range of issues. Having returned to Britain recently, she has placed herself in a position with which she feels comfortable.

Permindar has exhibited her work extensively in individual and group shows in Britain, Europe, Japan, Australia, Canada and America. Since 1991, the most memorable being the British Art Show 4 - a prestigious show highlighting the new and often provocative art of the last five years, organised by the Hayward Gallery which toured Manchester, Edinburgh and Cardiff in 1995.

Permindar Kaur

As a solo artist Permindar has been exhibiting her work since 1992 at numerous exhibitions and projects including a commission for the BBC as part of the BBC Billboard Art Project in 1992, "Regions and Growth" at The British Council, Barcelona, "Hidden Witness" at Galleri Amido, Sweden in 1994, "Small Spaces" at Galleri Isidor, Sweden in 1995, "Cold Comfort" at Ikon Gallery, Birmingham in 1996 and Galeria Carles Poy, Barcelona in 1997.

# Kanwaljit Kaur-Singh

Dr Kanwaljit Kaur-Singh, whose passion is to keep the Sikh traditions alive, was born in Amritsar, India in 1940. After completing her MA degree in 1961, Kanwaljit got married to a Mining Engineer Inderjeet Singh. In 1965, when their daughter was a year old, they moved to Britain for further studies which resulted in their settling here permanently.

A year later Kanwaljit decided to do some voluntary work in a primary school and began part-time teaching while both her daughters were studying. Having successfully brought up two daughters, Kanwaljit decided it was time to pay some attention to her career, initially taking the post of head teacher and then moving on to local authority inspector specialising in primary education. In 1990 she completed her thesis "The Contribution of Sikh Women to the Sikh Society".

Kanwaljit has a variety of personal achievements. She has been the Secretary, President and Chairperson of various Sikh and Asian organisations, contributed numerous articles on Sikhism as well as writing several of her own books including Learning the Sikh Way, World Religions, Sikhism, and Attitude to Nature, Women in Religion.

Kanwaljit has also worked successfully with the media, participating in many one-off radio and television programmes such as Heart of the Matter, From Where I Stand and recently Re-discovering Eve. She is a regular contributor to Pause for Thought on BBC Radio 2 and Something Understood on Radio 4, as well as other programmes concerning Sikhism.

High among Kanwaljit's other interests are interfaith dialogue, taking part in speaking and leading discussion groups and judging symposium competitions which have taken her on travels to different countries.

Currently Chairperson of the British Sikh Education Council, she has been a member of national Government organisations SEAC, NCC and SCAA.

# Anita Kaushik

Born in 1967, Anita Kaushik is a British female artist of Asian descent with "an implicit understanding of living and working in a multi-cultural environment"

Anita Kaushik

Anita's path to her present status as artist was not altogether a direct one. Initially beginning a genetics course at Manchester University she left feeling dissatisfied ethically and unchallenged. It was then she decided to pursue a career in art, which had been an interest since childhood. Due to inadequate funding in the arts field generally, her path has involved many supporting roles, such as: Indian vegetarian chef; waitress; cleaner' telephonist; day-service worker with people with leaning difficulties and / or disabilities; auxiliary nurse; library assistant; cinema ice-cream sales...

She graduated with a B.A Hons in Art and Social Context from Dartington College of Art in 1992. Her training involved her interest in community art and forms of communication in today's society. Her thesis *"The Sindy-rella Complex/Plastic Passions"* extensively dissected the Barbie doll by exploring the representation of women, racism, commodification, advertising and toys prevalent in western idealism. 'Barbie's' presence has weaved throughout her mixed media and public art practises for the last six years - inspired through her childhood. In 1996 for her MA in Public Art & Design, Anita took Barbie into Cyberspáce to explore an understanding of new technologies in relation to women, art, public spaces and identity. This work continues to be an ongoing project for her own personal research. She is currently pursuing a 'Traineeship in the Creative Applications of New Technologies in Community Contexts' at Jubilee Arts in the West Midlands, which is funded by the Arts Council of England.

Anita's work has been installed and exhibited at many festivals and public galleries since 1993. Her work aims to challenge dominant art theory, racism, marginalisation and to deconstruct notions of identity in contemporary Britain. In 1994 Shonali

Fernando, film-maker/writer interviewed and published an article on Anita in *Rungh* and *Fuse* two Canadian magazines. 1995 saw her painting *"The New Breed"* featured in the Channel Four documentary *"The Colour of Britain"* (directed by - Pratibha Parmer).

Anita co-organises and leads many community arts based projects as an enabler / facilitator. Her belief is that people can have access to and control over their own creativity and self-expressions so projects should be community-led. She feels that any project's process is just as important as the final product. Her training in this field has lead her to be multi talented in a variety of media and art forms: black and white photography, print-making, painting, sculpture installation, mural design and computer-aided work. Anita believes that the artists role is versatile, re-inventing spaces for contemporary public and environmental dilemmas. She also participates in collaborative work with other artists and other professionals, feeling strongly that artists should be centrally involved in planning for our futures and revitalising today's society.

# Mohini Kent

Mohini Kent, currently a journalist with India Today magazine, is also a film maker.

Schooled in India, she holds a first class degree in Psychology from Delhi University. After arriving in Britain, Mohini studied Graphics at Middlesex Polytechnic.

Regularly contributing to India Today Plus and India Today magazines, Mohini has also written for major Indian publications such The Times of India, Indian Express and The Week and Asian Age magazines. Her features focus on the arts and the Asian community, with special emphasis on women. A regular contributor to BBC 5 radio, she does a fortnightly round up of Indian newspapers, as well as contributing to Radio 5's magazine programme on current affairs.

Mohini's training in film had an emphasis on special effects and she has written and directed "Curry Tiffin" a documentary on Indian food, shot on location in India with commentary by Ben Kingsley, directed a feature length dance-drama of "The Ramayana" as well as numerous corporate videos and TV commercials.

Her interest in writing has led her to co-write a play with playwright Peter Terson and she is about to complete a collection of short stories for children.

Not suprisingly, Mohini's hobbies include theatre and opera, reading, walking and travelling.

# Lily Khan, OBE

Born in Baghdad, Iraq, where her father was stationed with the British Army, Lily Khan was educated in Baghdad, Dhaka, Calcutta, the US and Lebanon. She won a scholarship to the American University of Beirut and was also a Fulbright Scholar to Harvard University. She met the then Governor General of Pakistan Jinnah, as the representative of students in East Pakistan and was actively involved in the "Language Movement". A highly qualified individual with MA and BT degrees and a Diploma in Education to her credit, she was teacher, deputy head and principal of schools in the former East Pakistan from 1950 to 1971. In 1968, during the "Decade of Movement" in Pakistan, she was awarded the "Tamgha Imtiaz" Gold Medal of Excellence for services to education, by President Ayub Khan.

In 1971 Mrs Khan, her husband and two daughters arrived in Britain. She quickly became involved in voluntary work and was appointed Vice Chair of an East London youth club. She taught English as a second language and organised mother tongue classes in Bengali and Urdu for the Bethnal Green Adult Education Institute. This later became the Tower Hamlets Adult Education Institute and she took up the post of Director of its Asian Studies Centre. She also worked for the disbanded Inner London Education Authority (ILEA) and was asked by the authority to write the "Bangladesh Information Handbook", which is still highly regarded as a rich source of information on Bangladesh.

Amongst her other appointments, Mrs. Khan was the Bangladesh delegate to the United Nations, a Commissioner for the Commission for Racial Equality, is co-ordinator of the Westminster Homeless Families Project, a member of the BBC Advisory Board on Asian Programmes and Save the Children Fund Advisory Committee. In addition, she was also on the Burnage Inquiry Panel, an investigation into racism in Manchester schools, and was subsequently co-author of the book on its findings "Murder in the Schoolyard".

Mrs Khan is currently Chair of the Ethnic Minority Centre in Merton, an umbrella organisation which under her direction, has thrived to include over 70 affiliated groups and also chairs the Mental Health Project at the Marlborough Family Centre. She is closely involved with the Victoria and Albert Museum, London and its projects including Shamiana tent panel-making, Jainism and William Morris.

She has received many awards in world-wide recognition of her work including the illustrious OBE from Her Majesty The Queen in 1995, the Mayor of Merton Community Award and awards from groups in the USA and UK.

An extremely well travelled individual, she has lectured all over the world and is multi-lingual in English, Bengali, Urdu,

Hindi and Arabic. A grandmother of nine and great grandmother of one, her hobbies include embroidery, tapestry and gardening.

# Meher Khan

Meher Khan was born in India in 1950 but immigrated to Pakistan at a very young age. Getting married in her early teens, she came to London in 1966 with her husband.

Meher Khan

Looking for a flat to rent whilst her first child was a baby, they faced very distressing situations as the white landlords put up signs 'no children and no blacks'. Eventually, when they did find a flat, the landlord treated her very cruelly, making her scrub and clean the staircase with brush and soap and not allowing her baby to play with his toys or even cry. All these experiences caused her immense pain and made her think about the darker side of human nature. She could clearly see that there was no such thing as equal opportunities and the colour bar was in operation.

Several years passed before they were in a position to buy their own home, but in order to make the mortgage payments, they had to keep tenants, who also made things difficult for them.

After the birth of their third son, Meher decided to train herself and joined Adult Education to do various courses to qualify for a job. During this period she began helping local Asian women in her neighbourhood with simple tasks like accompanying them to the doctors, shops and social services. It made her aware of the difficulties of other women who suffered from language barriers and lack of education. One of the officers of the social services department suggested that Meher organise a proper group of women and apply for official recognition in order to help the community better. With the help of a few close friends, she formed a voluntary organisation in 1980 and named it the Muslim Women's Welfare Association.

It was hard work and time consuming but she carried on regardless of her frustrations and opposition and abuse from male members of the community.

In 1983 the group was funded by the Urban Aid Programme, giving Meher the opportunity to represent MWWA on various local Council committees and make friends with department officers. She also joined the Labour Party and worked hard for them, raising funds and encouraging new members.

In 1989 the Labour Party chose Meher to stand for election as a local Councillor. When elected, she became the first Asian Muslim woman councillor and, the following year, she became the first woman in the history of Waltham Forest to become Deputy Mayor.

As a Councillor, Meher has had the opportunity to be chair

of the Children's Committee, Vice-Chair of both the Leisure and Disability Committees and Chair of the Asian Centre Sub-Committee of the Council.

In 1994, Meher was elected as Mayor of Waltham Forest, making it the first time in the history of Great Britain that a muslim woman has been elected to this office.

Although the first woman on three occasions, the title she is proudest in gaining is that of grandmother.

## Qaisra Ehsan Khan

Qaisra Ehsan Khan

Qaisra Ehsan Khan, a Muslim socialist and feminist, was born in Pakistan in 1963, but brought up in Manchester. Her main concerns are community care, health and education.

She graduated from the University of Wales with a BA(Hons) in History and Archaeology.

After leaving University, she returned to Manchester where she spent a year doing voluntary work and a part time job in a home for elders. She moved to London in order to work for a local charity in Newham. Her career has involved working as a home care organiser in Newham, Southwark and Hackney. She has also worked as a youth worker in Kingston-upon-Thames and as a community care development officer in Barnet.

She joined the Labour Party in West Ham in 1986. She has been Conference delegate, Vice-Chair (premises), Secretary of the Women's Section, on the Local Government Executive Committee and Constituency fund-raiser.

Qaisra was elected as Councillor for the London Borough of Newham in 1994. She is currently Vice-Chair of Education, responsible for finance and careers service. A Non-Executive Director of Newham Healthcare Trust, she is also a member of the Socialist Education Association National Executive and Vice-Chair of the Newham Co-operative Party.

Qaisra is a member of Unison and was at one time a NALGO shop steward.

Her voluntary work has included being a trustee of Eastwards Trust Ltd and Newham Asian Arts Group. She currently works full time as a community care planning officer for the voluntary sector in Redbridge.

## Sandra Yasmin Khan

Sandra Yasmin Khan, eldest of three children, was born in 1962 and grew up in Wembley prior to the settling of Asians in the area. Her parents were working class immigrants who believed the only way for Black people to succeed in this country was through education. Her father in particular always pushed his children to succeed and achieve academically. Sandra studied at Alperton High School, which, despite being an ordinary state school, was Brent's pilot for the equal opportunities policy. Multiculturally diverse, Sandra's friendship group included Afro-Caribbean, Mediterranean, Asian, Jewish and Irish. If there was any racism, it must have been too subtle for a teenager enjoying life to notice. She does however remember how Afro-Caribbean girls were encouraged to participate in sports whilst Asian girls were expected to be studious and quiet.

Sandra Yasmin Khan

Leaving school with nine 'O' levels and three 'A' levels, she enrolled at London University to read History and Politics and went on to a gain a post-graduate teaching qualification.

Commencing her career in education, one of the reasons for which was her desire for all children to be able to have the same wonderful experiences of education as she had, she continues to strive towards this goal. As the only Asian female Head of Year in the school, she is responsible for over 300 pupils. Some of the initiatives set up by Sandra are parents surgeries and multicultural awareness, for which she was nominated Teacher of the Year, winning the award in 1997. She is also the teacher responsible for child protection at the school and has worked on a voluntary basis for the Samaritans, who are desperately short of Asian counsellors.

Sandra firmly believes that family support is the pinnacle to success, as is the determination to succeed and do your best in the face of British society's adversities.

# Swinder Kaur Khandpur

As a young girl, Swinder Kaur Khandpur watched her father build up his business from a small shop, "Oberoi's", to a local landmark on Southall Broadway. She began helping him from the age of 15 and eventually took over the business. As she loved her work thoroughly, her limitless energy and good management were the key to her success.

Swinder Kaur Khandpur

Educated to 'O' level standard, her learning curve has been steep while always knowing that she was up to the task of management. She became the vehicle for the rise of the business, controlling the financial aspects for the deals and making the best out of the acquisition. She found her work became her passion and, although she had support from her father and later on from her husband, there was no bright light directing her career, just a steady learning process which made her confident in terms of judgement and experience.

Every day at work was a fascinating and absorbing task. People, especially women, did not come in just to buy things but it had become a place where they were receiving a sympathetic hearing, advice and information.

The downfall of the Bank of Credit & Commerce International (BCCI) and ill-health forced her to sell her business. Having more time on her hands, Swinder pursued her education. Being interested in people, she completed a counselling course and joined a computer course to update her communication skills. She is also taking flower arrangement courses to maintain her creative and innovative skills.

Happily married for 22 years with three children and a well loved pet dog, she successfully juggles her time when running the home, pursuing further education and starting up a national charity 'Aid Asia' to help raise funds to support educational and health charities by selling secondhand clothes and other items.

With an eye for a good business opportunity, enthusiastic and enterprising, Swinder has spotted a specialist niche in the restaurant business and along with her husband is starting up a unique restaurant to serve the vegetarian community which feels left out in Southall.

# Razia Khatun

Razia Khatun was born into a middle class Muslim family in the Gaibandha District of Bangladesh in 1941. She was educated in Gaibandha and moved to Rajshani where she undertook her medical degree and graduated in 1964 from Rajshani University. In 1966, she married Dr. Abdul Quader, a Consultant Anaesthetist in County Durham, and joined him in Britain in 1969.

She began her career in Britain as a doctor working in various Paediatric and Gynaecological/Obstetric hospitals and went on to graduate with a Diploma in Child Health in 1972 and a Diploma in Gynae and Obstetrics in 1975.

Razia Khatun

After practising in hospitals for many years, she joined South Grange Medical Centre, Middlesborough as a General Practitioner and continues her work there today.

Content with having carved herself a medical career, she obtains greater fulfillment from having brought up two academically bright children: a daughter who also graduated in medicine and a son reading philosophy.

# Surendra Kochar

Surendra Kochar, an acclaimed radio and television actress, was born in the Punjab, India in 1938. Graduating with an MA and diplomas in Education, she qualified as a teacher but her interests lay in the world of film and acting. She followed her passion, successfully gaining employment with All India Radio and Television for over a decade, winning several national acting awards.

Surendra came to Britain in 1967 and continued working successfully in a profession in which few find work and even fewer succeed, especially those of ethnic origin. Working for the BBC World Service for 29 years, she would be familiar to those who watched "Gharbar" and "Make Yourself at Home", which was presented at Pebble Mill.

With a leading role in the first Asian television soap opera on Channel Four "Family Pride", she has also appeared in programmes such as "Common as Muck", "Moving Story", "The Buddha of Suburbia", "Hetty Wainthrope Investigates", "That The Butler Did", "Casualty" and "Coronation Street" and tread the boards in plays such as "The House of the Sun" and "A Yearning", as well as numerous radio plays and several corporate video films in Health and Social issues.

She will be remembered most recently for her memorable role in the internationally acclaimed controversial film "Bhaji on the Beach" and earlier films, including "My Sister Wife" and "Shakti".

# Kuldip Kaur Kohli

Kuldip Kaur Kohli, a development worker for Barnados, was born in Nairobi, Kenya in 1943.

Kuldip spent her childhood in Kenya, completed her schooling and spending two years at college, where she graduated with a diploma in teacher training. After working as a teacher for a while, Kuldip married Parduman Kohli in 1963 and joined him in India, where they spent the next three years.

In 1966, they emigrated to Britain and it wasn't long before Kuldip acquired her first job as a wages clerk, as well as looking after her new born son. She remained in the post for a year and then worked as a Post and Telegraph Officer until 1969, with a change of direction to Telephone Operator for several years.

Kuldip Kaur Kohli

When the family moved to Glasgow, Kuldip began her career in social work and with the community at large, initially as a helper to the Social Worker at the Church of Scotland International flat. In 1974, Kuldip moved to the post of School Attendance Officer for the Education Authority where she continued for two years. In 1976, Kuldip became a trainee Social Worker for the Social Work Department in Strathclyde. From 1984 to 1985, she was one of the Research Workers for the Glasgow Health Board on the Rickets Project. After working industriously, she moved swiftly to the position of Project Co-ordinator for Save the Children Fund, bringing much enthusiasm, new ideas and a fresh outlook. In 1986, she was appointed as a Community Relations Officer for the Strathclyde Community Relations Council and, through this post, became aware of the specific problems of the ethnic communities. Kuldip worked tirelessly with various statutory bodies to find ways of improving the service provision - the outcome of which was a success - with the recruitment of 12 social work trainees whose efforts were specifically targeted to those communities in most need.

In 1993, Kuldip acquired the position of Project Worker for Barnados in Glasgow. She worked specifically with the ethnic minorities and the disabled in the Asian community. Her commitment and dynamic approach to successfully organising projects and schemes was rewarded with a promotion to Development Worker. Developing new ideas and projects for minority groups, Kuldip and her co-workers received ,391,000 from the National Lottery for their "Apna" disability project.

With a constant desire to be in a position to assist needy groups in the community, Kuldip has worked with numerous organisations, GPs and Health Visitors to advocate on behalf of the Ethnic Minorities, the Gryffee Women's Home for Ethnic Minority Battered Wives as a Liaison Officer and Marriage Guidance Councillor and on the Advisory Committee of Blue Triangle Housing Associations' Sahara Group.

For the past 20 years, Kuldip has worked with charities on a purely voluntary basis. She states that all her work has been motivated by her belief in promoting social welfare for people who find it difficult to articulate their needs and her wish to empower ethnic minority people, especially those of Asian origin.

Kuldip is well respected among the various Asian communities in Glasgow for not only is she academically equipped for the tasks she takes on board but is also multi-lingual, speaking six languages, including Swaheli.

# Maninder Kohli

Maninder Kohli

Maninder Kohli, born into a warm close knitted family in Mhow, Madhya Pradesh, India in 1957, is a fashion designer and runs her own business.

Maninder arrived in Britain as a young bride in 1978 to a life as a married woman with no network of family support. Adjusting to her new environment was an isolating experience in the early years.

Struggling to make a marriage work that finally ended, Maninder was left to cope with two growing children. A natural entrepreneur with good costing and budgeting skills, she was quick to spot a niche in the ethnic designer clothing business.

Maninder began by designing and sewing a small selection of ethnic garments which were well received. This positive reaction encouraged Maninder to start a wholesale supply to a newly opened ethnic boutique in 1983.

Business continued to prosper so much so that in 1989, she opened a small retail boutique in the East end of London, aptly naming it "Khubsoorat". Maninder's sharp business acumen prompted her to set up a her own cottage industry in Delhi, India, to support the ever growing number of clientele. The five units were set up to specialise in fabrication, embroidery and the finished garment.

Maninder has formed a strong network of production and designing to produce a high quality product which continues to be well received by her clientele and in 1996, she opened the second "Khubsoorat" boutique in Wembley.

# Parveen Kumar

Born in Lahore in 1942, now in Pakistan, Parveen Kumar came to England in the mid 50s, and trained to be a doctor at St Bartholomew's Hospital Medical College.

After working in various junior doctor posts at Barts, Reading and Hammersmith Hospitals, Parveen returned to St Bartholomew's. A Reader at St Bartholomew's and The Royal London School of Medicine and Dentistry, she is also Honorary Consultant Physician at St Bartholomew's, the Royal London and Homerton Hospitals.

From 1991 to 1996 Parveen was Director of Postgraduate Education for, initially, Barts NHS Trust and later the Royal Hospitals Trust. Prior to that she was College Tutor for the Royal College of Physicians and a Clinical Tutor.

Currently the Clinical Sub-Dean for undergraduates at the new St Bartholomew's and The Royal London School of Medicine and Dentistry, she is also the Censor for the Royal College of Physicians and an examiner for the MRCP.

# Saroj Lal

Saroj Lal was deeply influenced by her father's fight for Indian Independence and his views on democracy and women's rights. Born in Gujranwala, Pakistan, Saroj spent her childhood in India at one of its most crucial times in history - Partition. Although born in what is now modern-day Pakistan, the family moved across the border at the time of Partition to India.

Educated in Chandigarh, Saroj completed her MA in Economics in 1962 and subsequently taught for a short time in Ludhiana. After getting married she moved to Madras and then Singapore, when her husband gained employment with Singapore Polytechnic. Saroj had her first taste of living in a multi-racial society in Singapore, where her son was also born, and then followed her move to Birmingham where Saroj

Saroj Lal

experienced racism for the first time.

Eventually the family settled in Edinburgh, where Saroj's second child, a daughter, was born. While bringing up her young family, Saroj managed to continue with both her education and career. In 1969 she trained as a primary school teacher and taught in Edinburgh until 1973. From 1973 to 1976 she worked extensively in a voluntary capacity with the YWCA and then as a community worker with the Roundabout International Centre until 1980. Her next move was to Lothian Racial Equality Council where she remained for 16 years, eventually becoming a Director in 1988. During this time, Saroj became the first Asian woman to be appointed as a Justice of the Peace in Scotland.

Working with the LREC has meant that Saroj has been involved in race and equal opportunity issues in a wide range of areas. This position gave her the opportunity to press for equality for black and minority communities through representation and negotiation with various bodies in both the private and public sector such as Lothian and Borders Police, Lothian Health Board, the Social Work and Education Departments and various ethnic minority organisations.

Although she has now taken early retirement from LREC, Saroj hopes to continue in actively supporting the work and aims of the organisation, whilst having more time to enjoy her home, travel and to pursue her interests in the Arts.

# Atiya Lockwood

Born in Lahore, Pakistan in February 1970, Atiya Lockwood is the Press Co-ordinator for Liberty, the leading UK-based humans rights and civil liberties organisation.

Atiya arrived in Britain in 1983 and after studying 'O' and 'A' levels, went on to read International Relations with French. She graduated with a BA (Hons) degree and joined Liberty. Atiya's main role is national spokesperson and in this capacity she has played a central role in publicising non-governmental organisations, submitting on UK's record to United Nations conference on the Elimination of all Forms of Racial Discrimination in March 1996.

Atiya is currently studying for an MSc at the London School of Economics.

# Grace Hermione Mackie

Grace Hermione Mackie was born in Badulla, Ceylon (now Sri Lanka) and educated at St. Paul's Girls High School. Her father was a well known society photographer and her grandfather was

Assistant Post Master General. She inherited her parents' love of music and won a Radio Ceylon singing scholarship in her late teens. She later sang on radio and had her own half hour programme, "In Concert Style", and a spot on Children's hour reading stories.

She married one of Radio Ceylon's popular announcers, who was also a jazz musician and had his own jazz group. Independence brought its attendant racial troubles; at one point, gang warfare became so violent that it drove a passing victim off the street into her house, pursued by a gang of men who chased him from room to room, attacking him and leaving him for dead under her dining table. This incident left her little children traumatised for months and she and her husband decided it was time to emigrate.

Grace Hermione Mackie

Unfortunately, once in Britain, her marriage collapsed and she was left to cope with the stresses of emigration and bringing up her three daughters totally on her own.

Grace worked as a Personal Assistant to Head of Personnel of a large manufacturing company for several years. Take-overs compelled her to seek employment elsewhere and she joined the Civil Service.

Grace re-married James Mackie in 1990 who, although English, was also born in Colombo, when his father managed Liptons, a firm for whom Grace had also worked. She retired in 1994 to look after her elderly father, but remains actively involved in voluntary work for the Association of the Blind. She also serves on two committees: the, Sri Lanka Women's Association in the UK, formed in 1946 by Lady de Soysa and Mrs Casinader, which aims to provide grants to six bright but needy girls in Sri Lanka, both secondary and career students, for a period of four years each and, in her capacity as past Secretary, President and currently Vice-President, she is constantly engaged in fund raising events; and the Civil Service Retirement Fellowship, where Grace's role is to provide monthly speakers for its members.

In her spare time, Grace has written several short stories and articles for magazines and local papers. Her love of her homeland started her off on her first book, a hardback "Of Jasmines and Jumboos", semi-autobiographical but also an insight into the social history of the Island in colonial days, with several authentic photographs. Published in Australia because of lack of interest from British publishers, the book is doing well. Supporters of her work have persuaded her to talk on the subject of Ceylon and this she now does to small groups and clubs.

# Mita Madden

Mita Madden, a dedicated and determined Training Officer within Social Services, was born in India in 1945.

Mita graduated with a BA in India where the main medium of teaching was in Bengali, with English a second language. On arriving in Britain in 1965 she had to take another Bachelor of Art. As there had been no real need to speak English in India, Mita found the task of doing a whole degree course in English quite daunting, but with perseverance came success and she graduated in English, Economics and Psychology.

Mita Madden

Her early experiences in Britain, sowed the seeds of her feelings that both overt and covert racism in Britain needed to be addressed. Today she believes in taking personal responsibility to challenge all forms of discrimination in society and has found it necessary to develop strategies to deal with it. Mita does not hold any qualifications in social work and has been primarily responsible for her own learning process. She strongly feels her lack of qualifications has not hindered her ability to perform her work thoroughly, though it has affected her career development.

After graduation, Mita got her first job as a social work assistant in 1971 and was married the same year. Her move into social work was not planned. Initially she had applied for a lower position in the organisation but because of her degree she was offered a higher position. In 1972 Mita left her job to have her first baby and then went back to work again in 1976, working continuously in social work until 1990 with only another break in 1978 to have her second child. Mita says her two daughters, who are of mixed parentage are well adjusted and comfortable with both cultures.

Since 1990 Mita has been in training. Unhappy with her role as training manager in the present management culture she now works as a training officer, focusing on adult services. Her main areas of interest are mental health, race equality and anti-discriminatory practice. Her aim has always been to work closely with psychiatric service users. Mita states that she owes a great deal of her mental health knowledge to her husband, from his academic and personal experience of having used psychiatric services. Together, they offer training on a range of mental health issues.

Previously, Mita was a consultant for the King's Fund on their Carer Impact project and has recently become a visiting member of the Mental Health Act Commission. She has co-written a chapter 'Training to Promote Race Equality' in a book entitled "Mental Health in a Multi-Ethnic Society" and has also contributed to the production of "A Cry for Change" and "The Survivor's Guide to Training Approved Social Workers" - Publication Feb. 1995 by (CCETSW) Central Council for Education & Training in Social Work.

As a 'carer' her contacts with Social Service professionals have unfortunately not been positive, though she has worked well with her husband's community psychiatric nurse and his consultant psychiatrist. During periods of crisis Mita gets her strength and support form her parents, her sister, her children and a few friends.

# Shameen Katharina Alexandra Mahmood

Shameen Mahmood was born in London in 1963 and, after early education and 'A' levels, was encouraged to continue into higher education. Attaining a diploma in Public Health and Hygiene in 1981, she studied Medical Physics in 1984 and completed her MSc in Biotechnology in 1989. In 1990 Shameen gained an Adult Teaching Certificate and attained a PGCE in 1993.

Commencing her career as a Cardiac Rehabilitation Officer, she trained in Medical Physics Physiological Measurements at Barts Hospital, before going on to be an Exercise Consultant.

In 1990 Shameen was elected Councillor for Waltham Forest, a post which she held for four years, and was appointed a Justice of the Peace in 1995.

# Meenu Maini

Beautiful and ambitious, born and brought up in India, Meenu Maini came to England in 1987 following her marriage to Rami a British-born Asian. As it was an arranged marriage everything happened so suddenly it was hard to take it all in. New relationships, new people and a new country left her cold and isolated. She felt her life was changed forever; separated from everything familiar and away from 'home'.

Since coming to England and being new in marriage was a huge upheaval all of its own, trying to fit in equally, she wanted the western sense of freedom with the warmth of the Eastern family. Living with the in-laws meant having to make compromises Meenu has developed an enormous admiration for her in-laws, who have the understanding to meet her half way.

Meenu Maini

After months of struggling to find her feet in the new environment, she found a part-time job in a community school, teaching Punjabi and Indian dance to children. This was the start of her interest in community work and arts and over the years she has participated in many Asian festivals and acted in three dramas, including Suraj Grehjan and Bebe Bilayat Wich.

Her hidden passion was to design Asian outfits for the young and, with the use of soft colours and aggressive design, she made an impact at many fashion shows she has organised. She takes this opportunity seriously and feels she has managed to find a special niche in the market, catering for young Asians.

Happily married with a young daughter, she feels that the years have mellowed her and given her a definite sense of direction and purpose. She often travels to India and Pakistan for her art and fashion shows and, although her roots are in India, she feels a great sense of belonging here, her adopted home.

# Nageena Malik

Nageena Malik was born 1964 in England and attained a degree in Medical Biochemistry at the University of Surrey. During her time at University she was secretary to the Friends of Asia Society and presented the 'Asian Hour' radio show on Radio Surrey.

In 1989 Nageena was awarded a Royal National Institute for the Blind studentship to undertake a three year PhD at the Oxford Research Unit in the discipline of Biophysics, the title of her thesis being "Ageing of human corneal and scleral collagen". After successfully completing her PhD she was awarded the first Post-doctoral Research Fellowship by Research in to Ageing. She continues to work for the Open University and is completing a Fellowship on the ageing of ocular tissues and effects of sugars, awarded by BT through Research into Ageing.

During this period of research, Nageena has been invited to speak at various academic institutes and conferences including the Nuffield Laboratory of Ophthalmology, University of Oxford, Moorfields Eye Hospital, London, the Rensselaer Polytechnic Institute, New York and an annual 'Crystal Protein' workshop at Daresbury Laboratory, near Warrington. Nageena was involved in a BBC radio show production about her scientific research project and has worked as a demonstrator and Course Director's Assistant for the Open University Summer Schools.

Her work relating to aspirin and the inhibition of collagen ageing received much press coverage and media publicity.

A keen member of an Oxfordshire health and fitness club, Nageena also enjoys pencil artwork and a combination of interests have led to her gaining a professional qualification as a make-up artist.

# Roshan McClenahan

Brought up in an atmosphere of intellectual freedom and tolerance, Roshan McClenahan was born in Bombay, India in 1947. Her grandfather and two of her female relatives were actively involved in the "Quit India" movement. Seeing strong women in her family gave Roshan the belief that her sex need not be a handicap in life.

Roshan came to Britain in 1965 and after qualifying as a speech therapist, attained an MSc degree. Marriage and two children followed whilst she continued to work, leading to a successful research and clinical career.

Several of her papers have been published in respected medical and health professional journals on stroke and motor neurone disease. She has also spoken at various conferences. In 1988 Roshan was awarded the Legg prize for research from the Royal Free Hospital and in 1995 was awarded the Foundation for Human Potential Fellowship to visit the USA.

Roshan McClenahan

Roshan feels her greatest achievements are marrying her husband, a man who has supported her all the way, and successfully juggling home life, husband and children as well as her career.

Her interests include theatre, economics, music and art, in particular the Daniell paintings of India. She is currently studying for a PhD.

# Rashida Shaikh Aliasgar Morbiwalla

Rashida Shaikh Aliasgar Morbiwalla, for whom spirituality is at the forefront of all she does, is a businesswoman and community teacher.

One of six children she was born in Dar-Es-Salaam, Tanzania in 1949, she is the daughter of the head of the community in Dar-Es-Salaam, the Dawoodi Bohras. Rashida had an idyllic childhood, was good at athletics and a leader in extra curricula activities. With a desire to further her studies, Rashida qualified as a secretary from an exclusive school of languages in London in 1968.

On her return home she married Shaikh Aliasgar, a Quality Control Manager in a large textile mill in Dar-Es-Salaam.

Rashida Shaikh Aliasgar Morbiwalla

When the couple moved to Leicester in 1974, she continued her secretarial studies at advanced level and was given a sponsorship to do Business Administration in Wigston College of Further Education. At the same time she had also opened her first clothes cash and carry. 1976 brought a move to Dubai where she worked as a secretary for the Brigadier of the Northern Emirates and as an Administrator at the Al Zahra Hospital in Sharjah.

Rashida returned to Britain in 1985 with the ambition to run her own business. After 16 years as a secretary, she took the plunge and set up Secretarial Services and opened an exclusive boutique specialising in Islamic attire.

When her time is not occupied in the boutique, Rashida is

busy doing a whole host of other things. Qualified as a religious teacher in Sidpur, India, she teaches religious studies to community children in Leicester. she also takes an active part in the community's women's organisations, enjoys cooking exotic Indian dishes, working out at the gym and practising massage and aromatherapy. Acting and singing in plays is another of her favourite pastimes.

With a personal desire to see women economically independent, one of Rashida's future ambitions is to actively encourage other Asian women to set up their own businesses either from their own homes or on a co-operative basis.

# Syeda-Masooda Mukhtar

Syeda-Masooda Mukhtar

Syeda-Masooda Mukhtar was born in Sargodha, Pakistan in 1963. She spent much of her childhood in the Gulf region of the Middle East and was sent to the UK by her parents at the age of 13 to pursue her studies. She graduated from the University of London and won the competitive MAFF scholarship to pursue her post graduate studies and later went on to complete her doctorate at Manchester Business School. She has worked on various high profile projects at both national and international level, mainly in the field of private sector development. In particular, she has been involved with and has developed various initiatives for development training for women both at a business start up level as well as for senior management. Her work in this field has been widely acclaimed and has gained widespread publicity leading to national and international media coverage.

A fellow at Manchester Business School, her background is business economics and information technology. She has a wide-ranging business and international consultancy experience which includes the Gulf states of the Middle East, the ASEAN region, the Indian sub-continent, USA and Northern Europe. Her areas of expertise include strategic development, entrepreneurship and economic policy. She specialises in business management training and has a particular interest in female entrepreneurship and technology/based firms. She has a number of publications and has presented at numerous international conferences. The co-editor of the book entitled High Technology Small Firms in 1990s, Syeda-Masooda serves on the board of NCHA Plc she was the youngest among the top 100 business women in the North West of England in 1993. She is the director for the various management training programmes. She lectures on these training and on the MBA programme.

# Zenobia Nadirshaw

Zenobia Nadirshaw has worked in the National Health Service for over 20 years and has a wide range of experience of teaching and training, lecturing and researching on mental health and learning disability issues.

Zenobia Nadirshaw

She has managed psychology services for people with learning disabilities and presently holds the position of Head of Psychology Services and Lead Clinician for Learning Disability Services with the Riverside Mental Health Trust in London. She has been involved in all services within The British Psychological Society on race and cultural issues, directing attention outside the profession at national level to the effects of social inequalities in the context of the mental health services and in the human care system.

She has spoken widely at national conferences, workshops and in the training and teaching of clinical psychologists. She was joint fund holder and joint author of the Double Discrimination publication in 1990 and On Women, Mental Health and Good Practice Training Pack in 1994. She has written and published widely on issues about women and mental health, women and learning disabilities and on race and psychology and minority ethnic communities.

She presently holds a grant from the Department of Health on work regarding clinical psychology and ethnic communities. She is the first Clinical Psychologist to hold the Chair of the Transcultural Psychiatry Society in the UK and has worked tirelessly in the NHS identifying ways in which minority ethnic people living in Britain experience disadvantage and discrimination in human health care services.

In 1996, she was selected for the Award for Challenging of Opportunity by the Standing Committee for the Promotion of Equal Opportunities, becoming the third successful candidate to receive this award, for the ways in which she has managed to contribute to this field and to the lives of people from ethnic minority groups experiencing disadvantages and discrimination.

# Kalpana Nandi

Dr Kalpana Nandi was born in Calcutta in 1947. Following her early education she chose medicine as her subject of further education, graduating with an MBBS and qualifying as a doctor. In 1970 she came to Britain and joined various training programmes. Progressing through them swiftly, she was appointed as a Consultant in Anaesthetics at Wolverhampton Hospital in 1980 and continues in this post today.

Kalpana feels very proud to be a member of the National Health Service in the UK and hopes to contribute in every way to maintain the ethos of the NHS.

# Surina Narula

Surina Narula

Surina Narula was born in Amritsar in 1958 into a family with an aristocratic mother and socialist father. From an early age, her father had instilled in his three children the need to care for the poorer classes, so at boarding school in Masoori, Surina's essays focused on poor children. Her election to head girl at school is where her confidence stems from today.

At 18, whilst still at college, the suggestion of marriage was put to Surina, which she brushed aside as a joke. Impressed by her challenging spirit on his visit, the would-be husband Harpinder Singh stressed to Surina that he wanted a partner in life and not a servant. Succumbing to the man who continues to nurture her growth, they were married in 1977. Encouraged by her husband and using the strength of the joint family environment, Surina continued her education, graduating with an MBA.

Returning to India from Libya in the early 1980s, she was shocked and stunned to learn of the murder of her two nephews and elder sister, a motherly figure and nine years her senior. Much speculation took place before Surina's family were able to prove that the crime had been committed by her sister's husband and his family. Through the process of bringing her brother-in-law to trial, Surina realised that justice had a price - money and the right contacts - a combination out of reach to much of India's population. This and the exposure to the 1984 riots in South Delhi, moulded Surina into a more determined and confident Sikh woman. Feeling the need to give something back, she joined the Indian Women's Organisation and actively raised funds. A move to England in 1989 for the education of her sons prompted Surina to participate in other charities. She chose to work with The Lotus Children, a charity based in the U.K.

Now an Executive Committee member of Consortium For Street Children, a charity based in the UK, she regularly visits the projects in India and has taken the cause to the Geneva Conference for Women. With a desire to establish the actual number of street children in Delhi, she has taken it on board to put together a method to achieve this. Her determination enabled the successful bringing together of the British and Asian communities for many of the functions she has organised to raise funds.

Regularly returning to Delhi, where she has an office, Surina has now set up the Hope India Foundation.

Firmly believing that sincerity in any aspect is what brings results, Surina is learning and absorbing as much as she can from politics and organisations in the UK, with the hope of putting it into practice when she finally returns to India.

# Aruna Nath

Aruna, born in Lahore, Pakistan in 1942, is a doctor with a string of letters after her name.

She studied first at St Thomas School in Simla progressing eventually to graduate with a MB, BS from the Hindu College in 1965. Then in 1968 at the Lady Hardinge Medical College in Delhi she gained her degree in Obstetrics RCOG. The next few years was a succession of successfully completed exams in London and with them the perverbial list of medical letters.

As a high flying doctor, Aruna is a member of numerous Societies such as: Fellow RSM, RCOG, International Society of Phychosomatic Obstetrics and Gynaecology, and the Medical Women's Federation, to name but a few.

Aruna has had many of her theses published, including The Problem of Cervical Smears, Family Planning 1974, The Effect of Prolonged Oral Contraceptive Steroid Use on Enzyme Activity and Vitamin Status, Journal of Steroid Biochemistry 1981.

No stranger to awards, in 1991 she received the Hind Rattan Award and then on consecutive years she won the International Women's Award and the Woman of the Year, in 1992 and 1993 respectively. She has an entry in the World Who's Who of Women and the International Who's Who of Contemporary Achievement.

When Aruna is not keeping herself busy in a medical capacity, she is involved in several social, religious and cultural societies such as the Bharitya Vidya Bhavan, Hare Krishna Movement, Asian Women's Association and many more. Her public duties have included serving as a Professional Secretariat on committees, Chairman National Women's Forum of the Overseas Doctors Association in the U.K, School Governor at Applegarth School, Croydon.

Aruna has successfully blended her career and her family life and her interests span across religion, devotion, social work, music and reading.

# Geeta P Nayak

Dr Geeta Nayak was born in Madras in 1947 and graduated with an MB, qualifying as a GP before emigrating to Britain in 1975.

She is the first Indian woman to be designated a GP Tutor in the UK and now works at the Royal Liverpool Trust and at Alder Hey Hospitals, as well as continuing as a GP at the Roby Medical Centre in Liverpool.

Geeta is a member of the LMC, St Helens, an Executive Partner of the Quest Consortium and a trustee of the Milap

Festival Trust, a registered charity.

Amongst her varied interests are medical education, travel, music and cooking.

# Deeyali Nayar

Deeyali Nayar was born in India in 1960 and studied at Loreto Convent School, Shillong. Attaining excellent grades, she gained entry to Lady Shri Ram College, Delhi University, where she was the founder member of the college film club, an active member of the Literary Society and also a member of the 'Wake-up Forum' involved in organising cultural awakening programmes.

Graduating as a BA(Hons) in English Literature with History and Philosophy, she went on to work for India's leading travel agent - Travel Corporation (India) Ltd in Lucknow, where she was responsible for international and domestic ticketing, inbound tour operations and selling outbound tours.

Marriage was followed by a nine year break in her career to bring up her two children.

In 1989, after her daughter commenced full time school, Deeyali successfully started a business in self-designed children's wear which involved designing, production and marketing skills. The pressures of having to spend more time on the business and having less for her children forced Deeyali to re-think, resulting in a decision to close her company in 1994.

In 1995 she joined India Mail, a weekly newspaper owned by the Business India Group, where she was solely responsible for planning and producing the women's pages every week, including all aspects of editorial work, covering original journalistic writing, sub-editing, planning page-content, designing layouts, proof-reading, liaising with typesetters and passing final page-proofs.

With her husband posted as an ex-patriate came the move to Britain in late 1995.

Currently studying for a BTEC Certificate in Publishing from West Herts College, Deeyali hopes to get back into publishing upon completion of her diploma.

# Lali Nayar

Lali Nayar, voted the UK's "Indian Chef of the Year" in 1993, is a home economist, television presenter, author and charity worker.

Born in Pune, India in 1946, she did her BA in English and History and also obtained a diploma in fine arts from Hyderabad. She arrived in Britain with her doctor husband in

1974 and settled in Newcastle-Under-Lyme in Staffordshire.

Initially, Lali worked as a part-time English teacher for three years and gradually involved herself with various national and international charity organisations. She became well-known for her commitment and efforts in helping the needy, especially for the brave trips she made to East European countries with medical aid. As with all success stories, Lali's first venture as a chef and cookery teacher had humble beginnings. She ran her Indian cookery classes from her own kitchen for nearly five years. As her reputation and confidence grew, Lali became a popular speaker and demonstrator at hotels, restaurants and organisations.

Lali Nayar

With her growing reputation came media attention and Lali has appeared on television on many occasions, especially since winning the "Indian Chef of the Year" title. She was TV Asia's cookery presenter with her own shows, Lali's Rasoi and Lali's Khanna aur Khazana.

In 1995, she presented a series of food related documentaries, "A taste for success", for Zee TV. In 1996, she was invited by Central Television to join their Asian programme "Eastern Promise".

Lali has written two books, "Who's Afraid of Indian Cooking" and "A Taste of Punjab". Her articles and recipes appear in various popular publications and she also made three videos introducing Indian cooking.

# Jayantee Nebhrajani

Jayantee Nebhrajani was born in Assam, India in 1937. After studying medicine and graduating with an MBBS, in India, she came to Britain in 1961.

Undergoing further studies and graduating with a Diploma in Anaesthetist and Fellow of Royal College of Anaesthetist, she was appointed Consultant Anaesthetist at Royal Hospital Trust, St Bartholomew's Hospital and at Homerton Hospital in 1972.

She enjoys reading, gardening and Indian and Western Classical music.

# Pratibha Parmar

Pratibha Parmar, an award winning independent film director, was born in Nairobi, Kenya in 1955. Pratibha arrived in Britain in 1967 and graduated with an MA in Social Sciences.

Her films have been exhibited widely at international film festivals and broadcast on television in many countries.

She has directed many ground-breaking documentary films which include Khush (1991) about Asian lesbians and gay men in England and India, which won three awards at festivals in Paris, Madrid and San Francisco, and A Place of Rage (1992) which won the Prized Pieces Competition for Best Historical Documentary in the US. She also produced and directed the documentary Warrior Marks made in collaboration with the Pulitzer Prize Winner Alice Walker. The film won two Public Prizes at film festivals in Paris and Madrid and enjoyed a successful theatrical release in the US.

Pratibha Parmar

The Colour of Britain, featuring the work of leading British Asian Artists and co-produced with Channel 4 and the Arts Council, was broadcast in 1995. In 1996, Pratibha produced and directed a documentary Jodie: An Icon on Hollywood star Jodie Foster.

Pratibha's first short drama, Memsahib Rita (1995) made for BBC Television featured Nisha K. Nayar and Meera Syal. In July 1997, Pratibha completed her second short drama Wavelengths featuring the actress Indra Ove.

In 1993, she was the recipient of an award from Frameline who organise the world's largest lesbian and gay film festival every year in San Francisco. This award is presented to an individual who has made a significant and outstanding contribution to lesbian and gay media. In 1995, Pratibha was presented with the The Pink Peacock Award: In Recognition of Exemplary Service to the South Asian Queer Community by Trikone, a South Asian lesbian and gay organisation in the US.

As well as working with a visual medium, Pratibha works with the written word, having edited and written several books including Warrior Marks - Female Genital Mutilation and the Sexual Blinding of Women (co-author Alice Walker) and Queer Looks - Perspectives on Lesbian and Gay Film and Video.

Pratibha is currently in developing with a feature drama with the writer/actress Rita Wolf.

# Sahera Pasha

Charismatic and vibrant Sahera Pasha, a Kathak dancer of versatility and grace, uses rich and varied rhythmic patterns, subtle gestures and expressions to portray the theme.

Born in Hyderabad in 1946 and brought up in Bombay, Sahera graduated as a BA in classical dance. She was then taken under the wing of the notable Guru Ganesh Hiralal who taught her the intricacies of the Jaipur Gharana Kathak style of dancing. Ten years of training has made her into one of the leading figures in Kathak dance. Through the years Sahera had developed a rich repertoire of expressions, perfected every hand movement and has an intrinsic command of the intricate rhythms of Kathak. She has been celebrated by the media for her ability of "Bhava" (expression) and her sense of "Laya" (rhythm).

Sahera has performed throughout India such as the American Bicentennial celebration in Bombay, 1976, the Ghosh Music Festival in Pannalal, 1977, and more recently at the 400th Anniversary of Hyderabad and a performance for the Vividh Kala Mahotsav Government of Maharashtra both in 1995. In 1977 Sahera was awarded "Singar Mani" one of the highest award of Sangeet Peeth, for her spectacular performance in the 16th Kal Ke Kalakar Sangeet Sammelan. In 1978 the Transworld Fair Selection Committee awarded her the "gold medal" . After charming a nation with her own inimitable style, Sahera toured the Middle East and then finally Europe and Britain.

Sahera came to settle in Britain in 1980 and at the same time gave her first performance in London at the Queen Elizabeth Hall. In 1982 Sahera represented India at the UNESCO International Festival in France where she was awarded the UNESCO Symbol for her performance.

Charity work has always been high on Sahera's work agenda, from performing for the flood victims of Bihar in 1976, the people of war-torn Chandigarh in 1982, she now performs regularly throughout Britain for a variety of charitable causes. Having given lectures on the history and techniques of Kathak Sahera now plans to set up her own Kathak dance school in London.

It is therefore no surprise that she has been seen by many as the "embodiment of Mughal Miniature".

# Bhadra Patel

Born in Zanzibar, now part of Tanzania, in 1940, when it was a British Protectorate under the rule of an Omani Sultan, Bhadra Patel grew up in a multi-faith and multicultural community. Because of religious tolerance in the island and its closeness to India, the Asian communities retained their cultural, linguistic and traditional values. Bhadra did not have the faintest idea that she would be able to use these values to develop her career in Britain many years later.

Bhadra Patel

Bhadra acquired her father's leadership qualities and her mother's compassion in her adult life and, as one of eleven children, she learned to respect, share and support with a strong sense of fairness. She also acquired her love for Indian music, dance, art, literature and languages by having this vast human resource within her family.

In 1957, Bhadra had her first opportunity to visit Britain as she was selected to represent Zanzibar Girl Guides at the World Centenary Camp. Her training during this visit enabled her to take up the post of Assistant District Commissioner for Thika District Guides in Kenya later.

In 1962, she graduated with a Bachelor of Arts degree from

Makerere University in Uganda and worked as a Graduate Trainee Librarian at the same university. She married in 1964 and joined her husband to teach in Kenya. Completing a post graduate diploma in education from Nairobi University, she was appointed as headmistress in a missionary government boarding school for girls in rural Kenya. When her first daughter was five, she decided to emigrate to Britain to study for a course in librarianship and perhaps settle here. Shortly after completing the course, she joined the School Library Services of the Inner London Education Authority.

Bhadra had her second daughter much later in life but, found her to be a source of comfort when she was widowed in 1986. Bringing up her two daughters single-handed was not an easy task, especially during their teen years, but she is proud that her daughters have grown up into respectable, educated and determined individuals.

Bhadra currently works as Librarian in Charge of the Multicultural Library and Information Service in Wandsworth, a multiracial inner London Borough. In her professional field, Bhadra has been a pioneer in showing others a way forward in providing services to minority groups. Her service is often visited by librarians from all over Britain and she feels that her success has been a result of all those qualities she had acquired as a child long ago in Zanzibar. During her 20 years in Wandsworth, Bhadra developed a Cultural Awareness Training Programme for librarians and, because of its success, staff from all other departments of the Borough are expected to attend it as part of their training to provide a quality service to their customers.

In addition to being a single parent, working full-time and, pursuing her interest in cultural activities, Bhadra undertakes voluntary work and in this capacity was a founder member of Croydon Asian Women's Organisation, where her main aim was to promote all women without discriminating their linguistic, religious and social backgrounds. She was also a founder member of Jyoti - Asian Women's Aid in Wandsworth. Her interest in education encouraged her to be a governor on the Board of Governors for her daughter's junior school for nine years, ensuring that issues concerning children from minority communities were never forgotten in all aspects of school life. Her involvement in Croydon Aashyana Project has managed to secure one housing project for single young Asian women, two sheltered accommodations for single and married elderly Asian women and men. Bhadra is also a member of the UK Asian Women's Conference and is trying to understand the working of the National Women's Commission.

With a special love for her mother tongue, Gujarati, Bhadra writes stories and articles for the ethnic press, translates information for statutory bodies and publishes children's stories in dual text.

# Hansa Patel

Born in Nairobi, Kenya, Hansa Patel was an Advocate by profession but a formidable woman with many leading roles.

Hansa's childhood was far from ordinary, her father being an illustrious businessman and a freedom fighter. She grew up in an environment that was charged with a fearlessness of the truth and a duty to serve and there began her ultimate aim to break down inequality for women. Hansa graduated as a BA Hons, MA., and LLB and shortly after launched her legal career in Nairobi. She later married Manubhai Patel, and their first daughter was born in 1970, the second daughter 1974. Her dedication led to her being voted the first vice-president of the International Federation of Women Lawyers. At the same time she initiated the present institution for mentally retarded children and organised its first Olympics.

Hansa Patel

In 1982, for the sake of their children's education, the family came to England. In her continual pursuit for women's equality Hansa continued to contribute on a voluntary basis and in 1987 became the chairperson for the North London branch of the UK Asian Women's Conference. During her nine year involvement she set up the SEWA Centre, a support centre for Asian women suffering from domestic violence, discrimination and related problems.

In 1990 Hansa joined the Management Board of the EC Migrants Forum which was responsible for promoting the needs of migrants. With the help of the social services Hansa was involved in setting up a translation and interpretation scheme in mental health, initiating facilities for interpreting on child protection cases and assisting in training social workers to use interpreters. With her progressive manner, she acquired funding to raise HIV awareness amongst Asian women, a subject which was and still is to some extent considered taboo.

With an abundance of energy Hansa was involved at grass roots levels while serving on the committees of Family Counselling Services and the British Diabetic Association as well as being actively involved in teaching English as second language.

Her passion remaining strong for the work carried out by the EC Migrants Forum, Hansa joined their Women's Committee as a rapporteur in 1992 and travelled extensively throughout Europe promoting the needs of migrants.

In 1995 at the International Women's Conference in Beijing, Hansa made a presentation on "The Right to Communicate", which is indicative of her vision to allow people from all walks of life to communicate their needs.

Sadly, Hansa died of a brain tumour in late 1996 and along with many others we pay our tribute to this powerful and dynamic women's rights campaigner who will be missed by all.

# Indira Patel

Indira Patel was born in Kenya in 1946 and was educated at Bondeni Primary School in Mombasa and Coast Girls High School in Nairobi. At the age of 16, she was awarded a teacher training scholarship by the British government.

At the age of 18, Indira married Bhanu Patel, a civil structural engineer in Nairobi. She taught primary school children form 1964 to 1975.

In 1975, Indira moved to London with her husband and two sons and in 1978 joined her friends in setting up the UK Asian Women's Conference to provide various voluntary services for Asian women in Britain and she remains actively involved in the organisation. She now manages the family's property business in London.

Indira has chaired conferences and seminars and has produced social and educational videos in five Asian languages.

Indira has addressed the migrants from (a European Union Consultative body in Brussels and in 1995, attended United Nations' fourth World Women's Conference in Beijing.

# Kanta Motilal Patel

Kanta Motilal Patel, has pursued a varied career, and most recent was the founder of the Greenwich Gujarati Group.

Kanta Motilal Patel

Graduating from University with a degree in Chemistry, she joined the Labour Party in 1969. Participating in community activities, student unions and the Labour Party she also became involved with her own community, teaching Gujarati at the Brent Asian Centre. This also entailed giving advice on welfare benefit, immigration and matrimony and she has continued in similar vein, as a voluntary community advice worker at the Indian Workers' Association in Southall.

A natural extension of her voluntary work led her to campaigning for the disadvantaged in the locality, in particular the elderly Asian, and unemployed with the Hammersmith and Fulham Welfare Rights Campaign.

Moving to Greenwich in 1984, Kanta was elected Vice Chair of the Asian Women's Art Group, She is a committee member of the Greenwich Action Committee Against Racial Attacks (GACARA), one of Britain's longest established and most respected anti-racist campaigning bodies. She set up the Asian Women's Group which provides creche facilities, refuge for battered women and young girls, day centre facilities for elderly Asians and confidential advice on welfare and legal matters.

Kanta studied for a diploma in Labour and Trade Union at South Bank Polytechnic. She was the first Asian woman to chair the Race Committee of the Association of London Authorities, and former National Vice-Chair of the Labour Party Black section.

In 1993, she joined SCORE (Standing Committee for Racial Equality in Europe) to campaign against the threat of Fortress Europe. Kanta is fluent in seven languages, including French, Swahili and Urdu.

# Lata K.D. Patel

Lata Patel, born in 1956 in India, lived in Uganda before coming to England in 1972. She studied Business Management and Accountancy.

In 1986, she was the first Indian woman to contest a local election on a Labour Party platform. In that year she became the first woman in Brent to be elected with the largest majority ever recorded for a candidate against an opposition incumbent. Two years later she was elected to the post of vice-president of the Hindu International.

Lata K.D. Patel

In 1989 Lata was elected Deputy Mayor of the London Borough of Brent, the first and the youngest woman ever to occupy that office anywhere in Britain. The following year she was returned unsurprisingly to her seat as a Councillor in the London Borough of Brent.

In 1991 Lata was awarded the Vishwa Gurjari Award in Ahmedabad, Gujarat, India in recognition of her services to the community in London. The citation for this award recognised, amongst other things, "her outstanding and meritorious contribution in the field of democracy, local self government, women's pride, human dignity and unity".

In May 1992 Lata became the first Indian woman in local government to be elected Deputy Leader of the Labour Party and, in June of the same year, the second Indian woman in the world and the first in Britain to be awarded the Arch of India Gold Award by the Non Resident Indians Institute in Detroit, USA. She was also simultaneously honoured with the Woman of the Year Award for selfless service to the community, and two of the country's most prestigious awards – the Mother India Award and the International Woman Award.

In 1994 she was elected with the largest majority for the third time on a Labour Party platform and the same year Hind Ratna and Nav Ratna awards, presented by the President of Indian for her work in the community. In 1996, her hard work and enthusiasm were recognised when she was elected Mayor for the London Borough of Brent, making her the first Gujarati Indian woman to be Mayor not only in the United Kingdom but also outside India.

Her home is used as her surgery for everyone in the community, people of all religious persuasions, colour, caste and creed. Here she gives guidance and counselling relating to personal issues, disputes and anxieties, as well as drawing on her expertise as an Indian woman in the world of business, to more than 10,000 people who visit her home each year. She always appears serene in a white sari although she works 15 hours a day. She is a devout Hindu, teetotaller and vegetarian, combining her role of businesswoman, public worker, wife and devoted mother.

# Vanita Patel

Vanita Patel

Daughter of a school teacher father and a grocery store owner mother, Vanita Patel was born in Uganda in 1956. The family emigrated to Britain in 1969 and, while her parents worked full time, Vanita had the responsibility of housekeeping and taking care of her siblings.

After completing her 'O' and 'A' levels, Vanita decided to pursue a career in teaching but, whilst studying for this, her parents wanted to introduce her to a gentleman Arindray with the prospect of marriage. In spite of ruling out marriage at the age of 19, she felt obliged to meet him because his mother was a friend of her parents and, much to her surprise, he convinced her to marry him within five minutes of their meeting.

Married six months later, Vanita did not enter the teaching profession due to limitations of her new found family, where daughters-in-law did not pursue any career outside housewifery. In keeping a positive mental attitude, she focused on self-development and starting a family of her own. She supported her husband in his private accountancy firm and his family business dealing in pharmaceuticals.

She soon had two sons to care for and became truly absorbed in being a good mother and wife. As soon as the children were in full-time education, she attended a number of classes at the Adult Education Centre, having the great advantage of being able to draw on the support and strength of her extended family.

Always with a 'mission' to instill good values and the importance of a solid education in her sons, she feels a great sense of achievement to have seen them grow up into fine young men. With both her sons in further education and her husband's businesses established, she was free to pursue something else that fulfilled her potential.

Her mother's qualities of patience, tolerance, loyalty and unconditional love for her and her family was pivotal in the next phase of her life. She reflected on her childhood and the traumas her mother encountered when her children became independent. To draw a comparison, where her mother grew closer to religion, Vanita turned to charity work. Introduced to Anti-Slavery International, the world's oldest human rights organisation, whose focus is to eradicate all forms of slavery and slavery-like practices, she was invited to join them as Chair of fund-raising. Thrown into a whirl of activity that demanded a great deal of her time, her husband and two sons suddenly felt threatened at not having automatic rights to her time. Guided by her own instincts, she managed to juggle the various roles in her life and her family are now avid supporters of her work.

Women of her generation were taught to be good wives, mothers and daughters-in-law, so she was always 'trying to please'. In an atmosphere of male supremacy, she confesses to falling into this trap, but through her work, she is able to voice her own beliefs and experiences about the atrocities occurring in the world today.

She feels privileged to be able to make personal sacrifices to help the plight of those less fortunate and it provides her with the resolve and determination to strive to work towards highlighting the issues concerning the charity.

# Madhu Lata Pathak

The daughter of a very well known politician who was actively involved in organising youth congress just after independence, Madhu Lata Pathak was born in 1945 in Hathras, Uttar Pradesh, India.

Madhu Lata Pathak

As a young girl, she had the privilege of presenting a red rose to Pandit Nehru when he visited Hathras in 1953 and was a member of the welcoming choir who greeted Dr Rajendra Prasad, the first President of the Republic of India.

Her early schooling was in Agra and Hathras and she was selected as one of the first batch of medical students at Aligarh Muslim University in 1962. She qualified in 1976 with an MBBS with several distinctions to her name. Shortly after completing her degree, she met Dr Suresh Pathak and was married in December of the same year.

They decided to venture out to see more of the world and, in December 1968, arrived in England, moving to Eire when her husband gained employment. Six months after the birth of their son in 1969, Madhu undertook a postgraduate degree at the School of Tropical Sciences in Liverpool University. Utilising her time at home, she also undertook postgraduate diplomas in anaesthetics and child health, during which time their second son was born.

Entering general practice in 1984 as a principal, she obtained her MRCGP in 1986 and, since 1987, along with her husband, she has been a trainer, devoting most of her time to develop a primary care team.

She was appointed Justice of the Peace in May 1976 at the Barking Magistrates Court, where she is now a senior member of the Bench.

In 1989 she was made president of the Inner Wheel Club of Goodmayes and her charity work that year involved support for the paediatric unit of the district general hospital and raising funds for several eye camps in India, which were organised by the Venu Eye Institute of New Delhi. In 1990, she was made the first female member of Ilford Rotary Club and has been Chairman of the International Committee, raising money for a water filtering project in Africa as well as the eye camps in India.

Since September 1994, she has been the Secretary of the Local Medical Committee which oversees the interests and welfare of General Practitioners of the Health Authority. With the active assistance of other GPs, she has started two out-of-hours Primary Care Centres in Dagenham and Romford.

Her latest addition to her academic achievements is a Diploma in Law, gained from Holborn Law College in 1996.

# Lady Aruna Paul

Lady Aruna Paul

Lady Paul, nee Aruna Vij, was born in Calcutta, India in 1936 in an Arya Samaj Punjabi family. She was educated at Loreto House Convent where she attained a BABT degree whilst also teaching at the same institute. She trained as a classical dancer and studied semi-classical music and art. As drama secretary, she produced, acted and directed dance dramas for local charities, relief funds and All India Radio. At a very young age, she gave voluntary help at Ram Krishna mission and Arya Samaj family planning projects in Howrah. She taught at Mother Theresa's Shishu Bhawan and Children's Welfare Home and later co-founded a ladies' study group of business men's wives and a Joytiermai Club which arranged education and study groups and also gave help and support to many poor and needy people.

In December 1956, Aruna married Swraj Paul. Twin sons, Ambar and Akash, were born in 1957, followed by a daughter, Anjli, in 1959. Their daughter Ambika, born in 1963, sadly died of leukaemia in 1968. Their youngest child, Angad, was born in 1970.

In 1966, Aruna and her husband came to live in London so that Ambika could receive specialised treatment. Her death, two years later, was a tragic loss. Whilst devoting time to her husband and family, Aruna, nonetheless, made time to help at the local hospital as a translator for ethnic minority patients and sick children.

In memory of their daughter Ambika, Aruna has built a hostel named after her for 100 children and a school for 1500 children, where she has been Patron for 25 years.

Aruna is a Patron of Women's India Association of UK where she introduced their main fund-raising function of the year. She helps with financial matters, organising auctions, brochures and general arrangements.

Aruna is also a Patron of the Arpana Charitable Trust UK. For her 60th birthday in 1996, she arranged a delightful lunch for her friends and, instead of presents, asked for donations to the Charity. She then doubled the amount raised and this has been used to build a Handicrafts Training Centre at Madhuban, Karnal, India which is already training and providing skills to many poor village women.

Aruna has been on the committee of Bharatiya Vidhya Bhavan and supported them for over 25 years and also lends her support to Future Hope, of which she is a Patron.

Through the Ambika Paul Foundation, Aruna and her husband help needy individuals and charities such as the NSPCC, Westminster Hospital, London Zoo, Children's Charity, The Royal Institute for the Blind, The Prince's Trust and youth clubs. Aruna works closely with her husband and fully supports him in all his activities.

In spite of her prodigious efforts on behalf of others, Aruna is reluctant to talk about her charitable activities as she believes in the Hindu principle of 'Guptdan' in which charity does not remain charity if you do not keep it hidden. It loses its value if it becomes self promotion.

Aruna has always had imaginative ideas and found novel ways of organising festivals and family occasions, such as Diwali or the birthdays of her children and six grandchildren. On her 40th wedding anniversary, she organised a tea and entertainment programme at the Nazareth House Old People's Home, where 64 old people from two Indian homes and English people from Nazareth House were brought together so they could share in the joy of the occasion.

Her greatest pleasure in life is to devote her time to her three grandsons and three granddaughters. For relaxation, Aruna enjoys hobbies such as flower arranging and food presentation, where her artistic skills are most apparent. Since a very young age, Aruna has believed in naturopathy, yoga, meditation and herbal remedies.

# Usha Kumari Prashar

Ushar Kumari Prashar was born in Kenya in 1948. She graduated with a degree in political science from Leeds in 1970 and went on to attain a Postgraduate Diploma in Social Administration at the University of Glasgow.

She took up her first career post at a Conciliation Officer with the Race Relations Board in 1971, continuing there until 1975. In 1977, she was appointed Director of Runnymede Trust where she made a significant contribution to the development of policy and practice in the field of race and immigration.

Usha Kumari Prashar

Shortly after leaving the Runnymede Trust, she became a fellow of the Policy Studies Institute and in 1986 became the first woman Director of the National Council for Voluntary Organisations and became an authoritative figure in the voluntary and charitable sector.

Since leaving the NCRU in 1991, she has held a concurrent portfolio of activities, some of which have included membership of the Royal Commission on Criminal Justice, the Lord Chancellor's Advisory Committee on Legal Education and the Arts Council of England. She was a Civil Service Commissioner from 1991 to 1996 and is currently Non-Executive Director of Channel 4 and Energy Saving Trust. Usha is also a Governor of the DeMontfort University and on the Board of Royal Holloway College.

In 1995, Usha was awarded the CBE for her contribution to public service.

A prolific writer, she has written and contributed to several books and publications and is a Fellow of the Royal Society of Arts and on the Council of the Policy Studies Institute.

# Kailash Puri

Kailash Puri

Kailash Puri, "an unwanted, unwelcome fifth daughter, with a hazy memory of childhood" was born in 1926 in Rawalpindi, now known as Islamabad, Pakistan. In 1943 she was married by arrangement (her husband's own initiative) to a handsome Sikh Paleobotanist. Over thirty years later, the belief that it was her husband's love, and encouragement to gain knowledge and accept challenges, reaffirms in her mind that living with such a brilliant and understanding man has given her "wings to fly".

They had three children and with her family she travelled through England, Europe, Nigeria, Ghana, East Africa and back to Britain, where they set up home in Liverpool in 1966. Nine years earlier, she had started up the first women's magazine in Punjabi "Subhagwati" which she was encouraged to relaunch in England. This was the first women's magazine in the language which catered for the emotional, physical, marital and family needs of Indian & Pakistani women. The first of many remarkable achievements, it earned her a household name and soon caught on in America, Canada, Singapore and the sub-continent.

Her career diversified when, in 1972, she became involved with a BBC television weekly Asian programme and started, along with others, a Yoga Centre, at which she taught three evenings a week. Here the emphasis was on a healthy diet, family stability and happiness. In addition, she was also working as a columnist and agony aunt to the Punjabi weeklies, Des

Pardes, Punjab Times and Sandesh. Through her knowledge of diet and nutrition, she became a consultant to Marks & Spencer and a visiting lecturer to Leith's School of Food & Wine. Experience gained in these diverse fields led her to be invited to give papers in various countries, including Japan, Korea, America, and Cairo and to attend seminars in India and Britain, amongst them Women of the Year in London and the Oxford University Asian Student's Union.

Kailash Puri is also a prolific and celebrated writer. Her first publication was a novel and short stories collection. Since then she has published six novels, three short story collections, three volumes of poetry, nine controversial books on sexology, three cookery books plus autobiography, anthologies and essays. In 1987 Kailash Puri was the recipient of the highly prestigious literary award - the Shiromany Sahitkar Award - made by Bhasha Vibhag (Language Department) Punjab Government. In 1988 Institute of Sikh Studies, new Delhi honoured her with Shiromani Sahitkar Award. In 1993, she won the Nelson Literary Award for her work. Her latest works, of which she is extremely proud is her autobiography "Bar Jao Lakh Beriya" published in 1996.

With so much to her credit, media attention has been plentiful. She has featured in numerous radio and television programmes, including conversations with Libby Purvis, Selina Scott, Mavis Nicholson, Sue McGregor and Robert Kilroy-Silk. Polly Toynbee interviewed her for The Guardian and she has also been featured in The Sunday Times, The Observer, She, Cosmopolitan and The Mail on Sunday. Her last piece of work in television was presenting "Dil Ki Baat", an advisory programme on T.V. Asia and she is currently writing two books and a weekly advisory column (agony aunt) "Aapna Aap Karay Deedar" in Der Parder Weekly, London.

# Anjna Raheja

Anjna Raheja, an ambitious Oxford graduate with high aspirations, is the Managing Director of her own Marketing and Public Relations Consultancy - Media Moguls.

Born in 1965, Anjna studied Experimental Psychology at Oxford University. After graduation, she started her career in marketing and PR in the leisure industry where she was responsible for the refurbishment and marketing of a top West End hotel.

It wasn't long before Anjna acquired the role of Head of Marketing and PR for the first pan-European Asian satellite TV and radio station - TV and Radio Asia. She spent the next two years developing advertising and PR campaigns for the channel, utilising her in-depth knowledge of the Asian community

Anjna Raheja

alongside her marketing experience.

With acute marketing foresight, Anjna picked up on the need for marketing expertise within the Asian sector and the growing interest from the mainstream market. Media Moguls was launched in 1992. Since its inception, the company has established itself as one of the UK's leading specialist ethnic marketing and PR consultancies, providing mainstream and Asian clients with the facility to structure highly targeted campaigns that accommodate cultural requirements.

Amongst Anjna's clientele are: The Aga Khan Foundation, The Commission for Racial Equality, The Royal Navy, The Asian Age, Eastern Eye Newspaper, Island Records. Warner International Records, and The Apache Indian Foundation.

Anjna has made a valuable contribution in changing the traditionally stereotypical way in which many men, and specifically Asian men, perceive Asian women. In the first couple of years she faced a certain amount of resistance within the male-dominated Asian market, but was determined to continue to prove her point. After four years, the company has made its mark and is growing steadily, proving that women are just as capable as men. The company's results over the last four years have placed it in a unique and enviable position, being regarded in the same light as mainstream companies, providing high quality, professional services from a dedicated team of young Asians.

Her drive and ambition to create a company that is a leader in the marketplace, providing companies with innovative and creative marketing and PR campaigns, comes from her belief that the Asian community should strive to remove the stereotypical images that currently exist within the marketplace, and prove that the Asian community is not only successful in the 'corner shop' trade, but in all realms of business.

As a second generation Asian, she believes it is essential to promote and develop the considerable talent and skills that exist within the Asian platform from which to develop their experience and expertise in a highly competitive industry.

# Sudesh Raheja

Sudesh Raheja, born in India in 1942, was brought up in a family with high academic ambitions. Fulfiling these aspirations, she attained two degrees: BA in English, History and Punjabi and a BA Hons in Hindi and later an Open University course in 'Ethnic Minorities and Community Relations'. As a child, Sudesh was interested in equal treatment of girls and women in society and this ideal has been one of the main focus points of her career.

Arriving in Britain in 1964, Sudesh's career began as an

Executive Officer at the Home Civil Service. After working in various departments she was promoted to Senior Executive Officer. During this period she was involved in promotion of equal opportunities with a wide range organisations, contract management contracting out and quality assurance.

She was a Race Relations Employment Advisor with the Department of Employment. Her brief was to promote equality of opportunity and eliminate racial discrimination in employment. This was the period when employers' awareness and commitment to equal opportunities was very little. She travelled around the country raising awareness of the issue and succeeded in convincing a large number of employers both in public and private sectors that equality of opportunity was all about good management practice and not something which was for women and minority ethnic groups. She was instrumental in persuading a large number of employers to develop and implement equal opportunity policies and practices. She supported organisations by providing training on wide range of issues including racial and cultural awareness, equal opportunities in recruitment and selection cross-cultural communication, equal opportunity legislation and so on.

Sudesh Raheja

Taking early retirement in April 1996 from her position as Careers and Guidance Adviser with the Department of Education and Employment she set a up her own consultancy, RAS ASSOCIATES, in a bid to pursue her real passion: the promotion of equal opportunities and the positive contributions of ethnic minority groups in Britain. In this capacity she has provided training for organisations including the Home Office, Metropolitan Police, Ministry of Defence and the Inland Revenue.

Alongside this, Sudesh has a whole list of other titles to her name: she is a Magistrate in Harrow, a Governor of a secondary school, Vice President for the Indian Association of Harrow, Vice Chair of the Harrow Police and Community Consultative Group, Vice Chair of the Racial Harassment Sub-Committee and a member of the Multi-Agency Racial Harassment Forum in Harrow. Sudesh is also on the Editorial Panel of "Savera" an Indian Association magazine and occasionally contributes to women's magazines.

Sudesh feels she has been very lucky to have had a husband that has supported her throughout her career and subscribes to her ideals.

In her spare time, Sudesh enjoys reading, debating social and political issues, entertaining and watching movies.

# Shama Rahman

Brimming with conviction and enthusiasm, Shama Rahman is a woman with a mission. An architect by profession, she swerved off the beaten track when inspired by a passion to put Asian culture and history into the mainstream.

Shama was born in 1952 and was educated in Bangladesh before proceeding to Alabama in the United States to complete her Bachelor and Master of Architecture degrees.

1980 brought another move, this time to the United Kingdom. Having completed her Masters degree in Computer-aided architectural design at Strathclyde University in Scotland, she settled in London, and with her husband set up Rahman Design Practice in Sheen, south-west London.

She put her career on hold to bring up her two children and used this time to join others in setting up the Women's Design Service, a group of community architects attached to the Greater London Council, which provided free service to women.

With her children in school, Shama resumed work as a Senior Lecturer at the School of Architecture and Interior Design at the University of North London. The job was comfortable, though too rigid to satisfy her desire for a challenge.

So it was that, sensing a chance to attain her objectives, she seized the opportunity to head the South Asian Studies programme at the university. As Course Tutor since 1994 she restructured the course in keeping with her ideas and brought into the university all the varied artistic skills and work going on culturally within the Asian community.

As a teacher of art and architecture, Sharma employs artistic experience as a primary source of intellectual inquiry. She experiments with communicating artistic experience through projects she calls 'storytelling', which integrate visual imagery and narrative with classical dance, in which she has also been trained.

Finally, through Rahman Design Practice, the architectural consultancy she shares with her husband, she is committed to meeting the needs of local Asian communities at a grassroots level.

# Harsha Rai

Harsha Rai

Harsha Rai, who has firmly believed since childhood that every woman should be independent and ambitious, has managed to carve her own professional career as a counsellor with EACH.

Born in Delhi in 1952, she was a keen athlete from a young age and represented her college gymnastics team, whilst studying for a BA. Pursuing an interest in languages, she studied Russian and Chinese shortly after graduating with an MA.

In 1977, Harsha came to Britain as the new bride of a successful doctor. Initially a daunting experience due to the adjustment of a new home and environment, Harsha spent the first 10 years bringing up her two sons. Whilst enjoying the status of wife and mother, she quietly nurtured and yearned to pursue her ambition to fulfil her childhood dream.

She began the first steps to her career as an advise worker with ACCEPT, a national charity for counselling people with drink-related problems, followed by a co-ordinator with Harrow Home Start for the development of service provision for Asian women.

Constantly juggling time and opportunities, Harsha's career progressed with sporadic support from her husband and children to her work as a counsellor with EACH (Ethnic Alcohol Counselling in Hounslow). This role enables Harsha to satisfy her need to work closely with people who come to EACH with a whole range of problems, whilst allowing her to maintain her professionalism.

In 1997 she gained her Post graduation Diploma in counselling from Middlesex University.

# Nina Rajarani

Nina Rajarani, choreographer, founder and artistic director of Srishti, carried out her Bharatanatyam training under Prakash Yadagudde at London's Bhavan Centre and additionally with Chitra Visweswaran of Madras. Since 1988, Nina has trained regularly in Madras under Mr and Mrs Dhananjayan. Apart from touring within the UK, Nina has performed extensively in Europe, Indian and the Far East, both as a soloist and as a duo with her teacher Prakash Yadagudde.

Nina Rajarani

Since 1991, Nina has been running a dance school at the Harrow Arts Centre, Middlesex, where over 60 students follow a six year examined course in which they are committed to two training sessions a week. Nina also teaches post-diploma students at the Bhavan Centre in London and is responsible for related administration.

As a performer, Nina and her company combine the South Asian dance tradition of Bharatanatyam with a contemporary approach to choreography, striving for creativity as its principle aim with an emphasis on being expressive, emotive and exploiting these qualities to address challenging and cultural issues.

Over the last few years, company productions that have been choreographed by Nina and have toured nationally included Hidden Forces (1996/97 - 24 performances), Utsav (1995 - 11 performances), Golden Chains (1994 - 14 performances) and Meetings (1992/93 - 15 performances).

# Sarita Rakhra

Sarita Rakhra

Sarita Rakhra manages an Asian Day Centre in Middlesex.

Arriving from Kenya in 1968, Sarita experienced racism at school, something that honed her determination to fight against injustice.

Coming from an extended family, where parents were emotionally out of reach she relied on her elder brother for support. It has been a long and arduous battle as an individual, she manage to find strength within her. In line with her parents' wishes, she embarked upon a career as a scientific researcher, although this was not her own first preference. She later went on to study for a diploma in Individual Psychology.

Marriage followed in 1977 and was the turning point in being able to lead her own life.

Passionately interested in the arts, Sarita is Chair of the Hounslow Arts Agency and co-runs Eastern Focus Ltd which presents discussion programmes on cable television.

She also serves on a number of committees and has jointly produced an educational booklet for South Asian drinkers with Alcohol Concern.

# Veena Soni Raleigh

Veena Soni Raleigh was born in Delhi in 1945 and graduated in Economics from Delhi University.

In 1965, she joined Cambridge University to read Economics. She obtained her MSc from the London School of Economics and went on to do a PhD in Demography. Her thesis was on "A demographic analysis of the sterilisation programme in the Indian States 1957 - 1973".

Working as an epidemiologist and specialist in health and population, she has established a leading reputation for her research into the health of ethnic minority populations in Britain.

Currently a Senior Research Fellow at Surrey University, her research into suicides among Asian women has attracted particular media attention. Veena also co-ordinates major national public health analytical projects, which her department is commissioned to undertake by the Department of Health.

Veena has always maintained an involvement with Third World health issues, focusing on women and children. She is a consultant on health and population to the Ministry of International Development and in this context makes regular visits to India and Cambodia to evaluate UK funded aid projects.

An external referee for several leading journals, including the British Medical Journal and a regular speaker at conferences on ethnic minority health issues, she has also worked with the

World Bank, the United Nations Family Planning Association (UNFPA), the Ford Foundation and University College London.

# Ravinder Randhawa

Ravinder Randhawa was born in a Punjabi village into a Jat Sikh family. Like many others of that background, the family had been uprooted during partition, suffering the same fate of terrible, fateful journeys and dislocation. Though the family resettled in India, the memories of that time percolated through to the next generation with some of the male family members emigrating abroad. Ravinder recollects her childhood in a small village whose connections spanned continents and in a family whose memory went back generations, containing heroes and heroines, villains and villainesses, weaving a rich tapestry of emotions.

Ravinder Randhawa

Having a kind of street-wise insight from living in a village, when Ravinder joined an English Model School, she was aware of the middle class snobbery of the teachers and their amusing conflicting reactions to her and a few others.

Arriving in Britain at the age of seven, she attended primary and secondary school in Leamington Spa and came to London to take her degree. Having had a passion for books since childhood, Ravinder always knew she wanted to be a writer, but also wanted to experience other areas of life before focusing on literature itself.

In the early 80's Ravinder began working for a group which wanted to set up a refuge and advice centre for Asian. She approached the work with dedication and idealism. At that time she was also involved with a feminist group, Awaaz, which met regularly for discussion, support and political work, on issues of racism, sexism, and violence against Asian women, identity and the exploration of differences between themselves and European women.

Taking up writing in 1985, as well as setting up the Asian Women Writers' Workshop, later to be known as the Asian Women Writers' Collective, her first novel, A Wicked Old Woman, was published in 1987, receiving an enthusiastic reception and getting into the best selling lists.

Her second novel "HARI-jan" was published in 1992 and also did extremely well, getting into the Feminist Bookfair's Top Twenty.

Ravinder has also written a range of shorts stories for teenagers and adults as well as for radio and television. Much in demand to undertake readings and talks in schools, universities and conferences, she has also contributed to non-fiction books, the latest being an article for an Italian publication "SOS

Razzismo", to be published by Feltrinelli.

She has recently completed her third novel Sita/Ferret. Ravinder is also a wife and mother.

# Vasanti Gangadhar Rao

Vasanti Gangadhar Rao, whose teaching career spanned over 32 years, was born in India in 1938. She attained her first class BA in Mathematics in Madras and went on to complete a BEd in Mathematics at Mysore University.

Between 1959 and 1967 Vasanti worked in mixed comprehensive schools in India. After her arrival in Britain, she became a mathematics teacher from 1969, Head of the Mathematics Department in various schools in Birmingham.

Progressing to Deputy Head at Bordesley Green Girls' School, a role she successfully carried out until 1981, her dedication was reward when she was made Head Teacher in 1982 at Handsworth Wood Girls' School, a position she maintained until 1990.

After taking early retirement in 1991, she has worked in the community as a member of the National Council for Women, Indian Ladies Club and Victim Support, and voluntary works with Imperial Cancer Research and UK Women's Centre.

Vasanti has a long list of personal achievements to her name, including: President of the Ladies Club (1970) and President/Secretary of the Asian Teachers Association from1974 to 1976. In 1982 she was invited by the High Commissioner of India to meet Indira Gandhi, Prime Minister of India at the time. No stranger to royalty, Vasanti was invited to the inauguration of the National Rubella Campaign in the presence of The Princess of Wales in1983 as a Trustee of the Prince's Trust she met The Prince of Wales in 1984 and in that same year was invited to a Garden Party at Buckingham Palace. As a supporter of the Duke of Edinburgh Award Scheme, she also met Prince Philip when escorting two of her pupils who were receiving their Gold Medal.

In 1987 she was made the Secretary for the Black Head Teachers and Deputy Head Teacher National Association.

In 1988 Vasanti was a member of the UK/USA Pilot study visits which was a follow up of Kenneth Baker's (then Education Secretary) visit to USA. As part of this programme she was invited to the White House to meet President Reagan. In 1972 she became a Trustee of Birmingham Ethnic Education & Advisory Services. 1993 saw her being appointed as a Non Executive Director of Good Hope Hospital NHS Trust and since 1995 she has been the Chair of South Asian Arts Development (SAMPAD).

Vasanti is regularly asked to give talks on a variety of topics such as Education, Multicultural issues and Travel and she takes part in numerous radio and television programmes.

# Sandeep Kaur Rapal

Sandeep Kaur Rapal, who works under the stage name Mona, composes, produces and sings her own songs.

Born in Hillingdon, Middlesex in 1978, she is the daughter of Channi, lead singer of the bhangra group ALAAP. Her love of composing, producing and singing was encouraged by her father who has supported her in all her endeavours.

A talented individual, she has received many awards and prizes for her participation in competitions and won a gold medal in the Brent Musical Festival in 1992 for her solo sitar piece performance.

As a singer, she has had many of her songs recorded and has performed live before crowds of 3,000 to 5,000 at venues including the Empire Ballroom and Hammersmith Palais.

Since completing her 'A' levels in Art & Design and French, Mona has been in full time employment with a major high street bank but still takes time out to compose her own pieces and participate in live performances.

# Zaibby Reading-Shaikh

Zaibby Reading-Shaikh, who's personal and professional interests range from health and social care issues to women's issues, was born in Tanzania, East Africa.

Zaibby's early education was completed at The Aga Khan Boarding school and in 1965 she came to Britain for further education.

Zaibby Reading-Shaikh

After graduation, Zaibby set up ante-natal classes for psycho-prophalaxis Asian women in Leicester in 1970. Still working with women in 1971, she was responsible for setting up the Domicilliary Family Planning service and was involved in health promotion with the Uganda Exodus.

The late 1970s brought a move to Middlesex and in 1978 Zaibby organised parentcraft classes for Asian Fathers in the Feltham/Bedford area. From 1981 to 1992, Zaibby was heavily involved with health promotion and preventative work with ethnic minority communities, in particular Asian women.

Zaibby was instrumental in setting up the first Asian Women Counselling service in Feltham at the Open Door Project in 1983. Since 1991, Zaibby has been the director of EACH (Ethnic Alcohol Counselling in Hounslow). With her leadership, EACH has gone from strength to strength and in 1993 was awarded a Good Practice Certificate by the Department of Health. One of the leading ethnic minority counselling services in Britain, EACH has also received recognition from the department of Health and Social Services Inspectorate.

Under Zaibby's guidance, EACH has expanded from Hounslow to the London Boroughs of Hammersmith & Ealing and has set up new offices in Harrow and extended its services to Hillingdon. In 1996, EACH received funding from the National Lottery Charities Board to develop a re-skilling and re-employment project.

On behalf of EACH, Zaibby now provides training and consultancy on health and social care issues and on developing new services for the ethnic communities.

Zaibby has been involved in the development and management of a wide range of other local and national Asian community organisations, either as an executive committee member or a volunteer and is also a qualified family therapist, practice teacher and clinical supervisor.

# Ragini Reddy

Ragini Reddy

Ragini Reddy, was born and brought up in Hyderabad, India. Achieving excellent grades in school, she went on to Osmania Medical College and gained her MBBS degree in 1982.

Ragini married Raj in 1984 and they moved to Britain to pursue their education in the same year. Ragini gained post-graduation in Obstetrics and Gynaecology in 1985. After an initial struggle she found good career opportunities in Birmingham.

A specialist in the problem of infertility, she has contributed articles to academic journals and takes every opportunity to participate in national and international conferences on the subject.

At present Ragini is working as a Senior Registrar in Obstetrics and Gynaecology and is eager to progress to a Consultants post in the West Midlands.

# DJ Ritu

DJ Ritu, a vibrant London based DJ and radio presenter, well known for her expertise in modern UK-produced Asian music, was born in London.

She graduated with a BA (Hons) degree in Fine Art and, since completing a Postgraduate Diploma in Youth and Community Work, has worked as a DJ in the mainstream club scene.

Having started out as a 'chart music DJ', Ritu went on to hold residencies at the Paradise Club, Ormonds and The Mambo Inn to name but a few. She became resident DJ at

London's first successful weekly Asian nightclub, 'Bombay Jungle' at the Wag Club, London, and is currently resident at clubs such as 'The End', 'The Dome' and 'HQs' in London and frequently guests at a variety of other clubs.

In 1992, DJ Ritu began working in radio with her own weekly Bhangra programme, 'Bhangra in Beds', for BBC 3 Counties Radio, and presented programmes for a temporary London Brazen Radio where her daily programme, 'Spin the Globe', received the highest ratings for the station. The first Asian DJ invited to play on London's KISS 100 FM radio station, she has produced and presented three hour mix programmes for the 'Giving It Up' slot, and featured in the cult nightclub programme 'BPM'.

DJ Ritu

DJ Ritu currently presents a weekly Asian music programme on BBC World Service called 'Bhangrabeat', pioneering the progress of Bhangra and Asian underground music and sending it world-wide to a non-Asian audience. She has co-set up the new Asian fusion label 'Outcaste Records', becoming head of A&R, signing key acts Nitin Sawhney and Badmarsh. Outcaste has been instrumental in propelling the sound of the British Asian 'underground' scene forward. Ritu's club and radio work over the last three years is an extension of this and she is one of the key DJs on this scene.

Ritu works abroad extensively, DJ-ing in clubs in Canada, Holland, Austria, Germany, Japan, Slovenia, France and Belgium, predominantly taking Asian sounds to new international audiences.

As well as her work in the music business, she continues as a Senior Youth Worker for the London Borough of Haringey.

Sheer stamina and perseverance gives Ritu confidence to develop skills to survive in a very competitive male dominated industry.

# Bharati Roy

Bharati Roy was born in Calcutta, India, in 1953. Graduating from Calcutta University with a BA degree, she then acquired a professional qualification in Social Work and Community Development.

She arrived in Britain in 1981 and added a Certificate in teaching ESOL at the City & Guilds of London Institute and then a qualification in Community Interpreting from the Lambeth Community Education Department to her existing qualifications.

Bharati Roy

Bharati works for Brighton Health Care and discusses ethnic minority issues on BBC Radio Sussex. She helped to produce a video on the problems of 'Bangladeshi women in Brighton' for the Light House Video Centre.

In addition to her role as a Community Education tutor and Community Interpreter, Bharati is also a Home/School Liaison Officer.

# Sarita Sabharwal

Sarita Sabharwal

Born and brought up in Delhi, India, Sarita Sabharwal is a well known radio and television presenter and the face promoting many famous brands of Asian foods in television and advertising campaigns.

Graduating from Delhi University in English, Hindi, Economics and Political Science, she pursued her personal interest of music, dance and drama by obtaining a Diploma in vocal classical music from Allahabad.

An active individual, she was a cadet with the National Cadet Corps.

Her first opportunity to put her musical theory into practice came with a five year appointment as a singer and drama artist for the All India Radio youth programme.

It was during this time that Sarita met a supportive and co-operative Ramesh whom she later married and confesses that today he is still the man of her dreams.

Shortly after marriage, the couple arrived in London for permanent settlement. Blessed with three lovely children, Sarita commenced her career in administration moving on to presenting and producing her own programmes for Sunrise and Radio Asia and then researching and hosting the morning breakfast programme for TV Asia. In 1994, she also presented Aap Ki Farmaish for Zee TV and is presently presenting two shows for Cable television network Namaste.

Recognition for her services to the community, she was awarded Namaste Gold by the School of Cultural Heritage in 1992, a community award from the Asian Film Academy and best female presenter in the Asian DJ awards in 1993 and a community award from the Indian Council of World Affairs in 1994.

Promoting her culture and values through her promotion and production company, S.R. Arts, Sarita gains personal enjoyment from comparing shows and helping out at charity events as well as taking the role of housewife in many television commercials.

# K. Sultana Saeed

K. Sultana Saeed, a law lecturer was born into an old well established family in Lucknow, India.

Having studied at Poona and Bombay Universities, she applied for and won a Full bright Scholarship to the USA but chose to come to Britain to continue her education.

Arriving in 1956 in the middle of Suez crisis, Sultana studied International Law and International Relations. In 1967 she received her PhD and that same year was appointed lecturer in Law at University College London, where she specialised in public law, criminology, criminal and juvenile justice until 1989.

As a visiting scholar at the Institute of Criminology in Cambridge from 1988-1990, Dr Saeed set up and conducted a pilot study into "Behaviour Modification of School children". In 1988 she was made Honorary Research Fellow of the Department of Islamic Arabic studies at the University of Exeter and then in 1994, Fellow of Selly Oak College in Birmingham.

K. Sultana Saeed

Sultana has been a committed member of many professional organisations. In the 1970s she became a founder member of the International Society of Victimology. She has been an active member of Justice, a council member of the Institute for the Study and Treatment of Delinquency (1988 to present), Member of the Parole Board for England and Wales (1985-1988), Member of the General Advisory Council of the BBC (1991 to 1996), Council Member of the British Society of Criminologists (1993-1996), Council Member of International Social Service, Member of the Advisory Committee on Genetic Testing (1996 to present), Non-Executive Director of an NHS trust, and a member of various committees connected with the Convocation of the University of London.

Sultana's published articles are, " Drunken Drivers: A New Approach" (Police Journal 1982), "Lessons of Brixton" (Journal of Public Law 1982), "Attitude of Asian Children to Police" (The New Community 1982) and "Political Crime: Legal and Criminological Perspective", presented to the University of Warsaw.

She has been a guest lecturer and speaker at many international conferences and academic institutions, including in the Netherlands and China.

Sultana has a particular interest in actively pursuing Inter-faith Understanding, a field in which she believes women to be are very central.

Sultana, now a doctor and a journalist respectively, married with two daughters and a supportive husband, she has always successfully juggled her time between looking after a husband, young family, a full time career and her home.

Her hobbies include meditation, listening to famous old singers of Ghazals and Bhajans, theatre and Indian classical dance.

# Jaee Samant

Jaee Samant, one of the few Asian women in the fast stream of the British Civil Service, was born in Bombay, India in 1967.

On arriving in Britain in 1980, Jaee went to the Henrietta Barnet School where she excelled at her academic studies as well

Jaee Samant

as being the form captain and editor of the school magazine. In 1985 she won the Henrietta Barnet Bequest Award.

Her academic success lead her straight to Oxford University where she completed an MA Modern History While at Oxford, Jaee participated in numerous extra curricular activities. In 1986 she spoke at the Oxford Union Debating Society as part of a Guinness Record for the longest debate. In that same year Jaee was in the University Dramatic Society's production of "Macbeth". As Chairperson for the "Mansfield 2000" Appeal and Development Plan in 1987, she organised a Winter Ball at Oxford to raise funds for the Appeal.

Jaee has also done her share of voluntary work. In 1983 she worked at "Friends of the Earth" and alongside her father Dr. J. D. Samant in a leper treatment home in Bombay in the same year and again in 1985. In 1990 she worked on a farm in South India.

Jaee feels that one of her greatest achievements was being selected for the Civil Service Fast Stream. She was made Private Secretary to the Rt. Hon. Michael Portillo, Secretary of State for Employment and was Private Secretary to Rt. Hon. Gillian Shepherd, Secretary of State for Education and Employment.

She is now advising Education and Employment ministers on the "welfare to work" deal, a labour government initiative.

Jaee's interests include reading, theatre & cinema, music, travel and dinning out.

# Shaila Samant

Shaila Samant

Shaila Samant, the daughter of the well-known physician and social worker, the late Dr YA Samant, in whose memory a prominent square was named in the heart of Mumbai (Bombay), was born in Indian City in 1940.

Shaila graduated as a Bachelor of Science as well as a Bachelor of Laws from the University of Bombay and won several prizes in badminton, kabadi and swimming in school and college tournaments. In 1964, she married Mr KL Samant, Secretary, Board of Directors, Bank of India, Bombay. Due to her husband's postings, Shaila lived in Singapore for five years, Japan for a year and Hong Kong for three years, before arriving in Britain at the beginning of 1980.

Shaila has contributed articles and short stories to several English and Marathi magazines in India. She also plays bridge and has won many prizes in competitions held in Mumbai, Singapore, Hong Kong, London and Cyprus.

Currently, an executive officer in the Home Office, Shaila is a firm believer in academic attainment and instilled this belief into her children, who are both Oxford graduates.

# Daljit Sandhu

An activist around issues concerning Black women and a feminist, Daljit Sandhu was born in London in 1964. She graduated from university with a BSc degree and at present is a Housing Services Manager in Special Needs Housing Association.

Daljit Sandhu

The youngest daughter in a family of two sisters and a brother, she was well aware that girls were treated differently. Although a lot of emotional energies were invested in them during their upbringing, she felt that her brother got away with a lot more, which resulted in her being closer to her mother and two sisters. She identified with the difficulties tied in with cultural and religious pressures which impinge on the choices she could make.

Throughout her adolescence, she found a mixed cultural upbringing confusing and had to fight much harder to prove herself. Struggling to find identity and sexuality on her own terms, the search for self derived from a combination of sources tugging in completely opposite directions. She strongly believes expectations of relationships are natural rather than prescribed or constructed and hence refused to give in to marriage.

She feels her political identity is British while her personal identity is Indian. There are strong links with India but she has created a niche for herself here. Confident, independent and rebellious, Daljit's interest and expertise is in the field of women's issues. Her work focuses on campaigning and fighting for justice in the cases of women experiencing domestic violence.

Passionate about sports, she played hockey for England and also represented London teams in volleyball and softball locally and abroad.

It is difficult to label her for she is a complicated woman. A controversial and challenging yet self contained warm personality puts her in a league of her own.

# Rita Sanghrajka

Rita Sanghrajka was born in Zanzibar and educated in an English medium school until 1964, when Zanzibar which was ruled by an Omani sultanate, was involved in a civil war, supported by mainland Tangayika (now Tanzania). Shortly after the war, Rita's father was transferred to other parts of Tanzania because of his position in the banking profession.

Rita and her family came to London on holiday in the early 1970s. They did not intend to settle here but, were forced by the political events. Familiarised and beginning to settle, Rita attended college to complete a secretarial course with additional 'O' levels. Commencing her career as a secretary in an advertising company, she progressed to become a PA to the Marketing Director of a Shipping Company, and beginning to settle here in Britain.

Marriage followed in the late 1970s to a Chemical Engineer working in the oil industry. Rita had two children and settled into the role of housewife. In late 1980s her husband's career took a turn as he started his first assignment in Scotland. Having spare time on her hands, she became involved in helping the local school to raise money for charities by organising bazaars and outings for children. By the early 1990s, her husband had been posted to Brunei in the Far East, so she took up additional responsibilities by helping to organise, and participate in field activities, geographical surveys and social events, taking the school children on camping expeditions, one of which included a visit to the Sultan of Brunei's wife's palace. Rita also went on a jungle survival trip with the Gurkha Army, which involved walking through the jungle, abseiling and rifle shooting, and took part in a readers' group where each member was asked either to read or remember a part they were portraying. This group performed for children and adults.

As Rita enjoyed working with young children, she pursued her career as Learning Assistant in Special Needs by gaining relevant further education. Now working in a High School Special Unit, she assists dyslexic children with literacy and numeracy skills as well as empowering them to be independent in the mainstream of the school. She also helps children to focus on their school and homework by setting their tasks out in such a way that they will be able to manage the work by themselves, prepares them for life outside of school by teaching them life skills such as writing a Curriculum Vitae, talking through job experience, money matters and learning to drive as well as co-ordinating with the examination boards on getting permission for students to get special dispensation for their SATS, GCSEs and other examinations, all of which is very important for students who are slower than their peers.

Rita also give special consideration to students and parents of bi-lingual students who need to communicate with the school in Gujrati whenever necessary.

# Zubedah Sarwar

Zubedah Sarwar, a Health Educator, was born in Pakistan in 1951 and arrived in Britain at the tender age of three months. Brought up in Newcastle until the age of five, her family moved to Doncaster where she began her schooling.

Graduating with a certificate in Health Education, she gained employment as a Health Educator for a general practice. Focusing particularly on the health of Asian women, she has been able to continue her skills in training health professionals in Asian culture and diet. Through the knowledge and experience gained, she has been able to compile a publication entitled "Health on Asian Diet" and has gained numerous qualifications in Health Studies, finding research work particularly interesting.

Zubedah Sarwar

Zubedah has been the Vice Chairperson of the Joint Equal Opportunities Sub-committee of the Nottinghamshire County Council and was the first Muslim woman to be selected as a Magistrate, holding the post for nine years.

She states that, with the love and support of her husband Mohammed, she has been able to put her skills and knowledge to good use, by helping the ethnic community in Nottingham through her role as a part-time interpreter, a position she had held for the last five years, a health educator at a GP practice for four years and involvement in a vocational training scheme for GP registrars.

Awarded the Nursing Community Magazine 3M award for a project in post natal depression in Asian women, she is also recorded in the Asian Who's Who International publication.

The proud mother of a daughter who is a dietician, a son who is a doctor and another son and daughter who are still studying, Zubedah feels the most important aspect of her life is her close knit family.

# Yashveer Sathi

Yashveer Sathi was born in 1941 in Bari Sadri, Rajasthan, India.

She graduated with a MA in History and a diploma in Education and taught history in The Government College for Boys and the Government College for Women in Ludhiana.

Yashveer Sathi

Yashveer came to Britain in 1966 as a young bride. A determined individual, she overcame feelings of isolation to carve out a teaching career soon after her arrival. She insisted on wearing sari both to work and social gatherings.

Since leaving teaching in 1990, Yashveer has remained involved in education, initially as chair of a board of school governors and currently as a vice-chair.

Currently a company director. She is actively involved in community work and is also a member of the Labour Party, she co-runs the company with her husband. Her love for literator, arts and book keeps her in touch with her artistic side of herself which she values tremendously.

# Dolly Saxena

Dolly Saxena was born in Lucknow, India in 1932. Studying medicine at Agra Medical College, India she attained her MMBS in 1958.

Dolly arrived in England in 1959 and began practising as a General Practitioner, continuing with further training to qualify as a Family Planning Instructor.

In 1980 Dolly opened a Health and Beauty Clinic and since has achieved a certificate in Beauty Therapy and a certificate in Advanced Electrology.

In 1987 Dolly became the Secretary of the Indian Medical Association and was appointed President in 1994, a position she held for two years. In 1980 she became the Assistant Secretary of the Overseas Development Association - metropolitan branch and after 10 years was made Vice Chair and is a Fellow of the ODA in the UK Ltd.

She enjoys photography, fashion, designing, painting, swimming, travelling and community work.

# Perminder Sekhon

Perminder Sekhon was born and brought up in Southall, Middlesex.

Perminder Sekhon

She studied English and Drama in an Further Education college in Lancashire and began her career in theatre at the age of 25, prior to which she had focused her energies in working in Asian women's refuges in London and Birmingham.

Perminder started acting in community Asian drama workshops in 1993 and gradually began to write and perform her own material.

She has since set up her own company Mehtab Theatre, which works in bi-lingual medium, delivering innovative and inspiring Punjabi and English work on issues concerning race, gender, class and sexuality.

As a performer, she has received much media attention, as well as critical acclaim from the likes of The Stage magazine, which stated "A critical unsentimental examination from the inside of British Asian culture, the Indian diaspora has found an eloquent voice in Sekhon".

In addition to her performance work, Perminder is also a photographer and focuses her work on issues regarding sexual health, homophobia and identity. Her portrayal of these issues has been used in many poster campaigns.

Remaining in touch with the community at large, she has been a women's sexual health worker since 1993, with the NAZ project, an HIV and AIDS agency.

Perminder is currently in discussion with a national

television network for the dramatisation of the play Madhuri I Love You.

# Robina Shah

Robina Shah was born in England in 1964. Since attaining a BSc and a MSc in Psychology she has worked as a psychologist, independent trainer and consultant.

She is the author of The Silent Minority Children, Asian Children With Disabilities and the co-author of People with Learning Disabilities. She has also written numerous articles for health and social work journals.

Robina is a member of the Mental Health Foundation Learning Disabilities Committee, the Joseph Rowntree Trust Foundation and others.

Other positions which she holds currently include Non-Executive Director of the Greater Manchester Ambulance Service, NHS Trust and Justice of the Peace for Manchester Inner City Bench.

Her personal interests include rambling, writing poetry and squash.

# Sharanjeet Shan

With a diverse and satisfying teaching career that spans over 27 years, Sharanjeet Shan is Executive Director of a Mathematics Centre for Primary Teachers.

Born in India in 1945, Sharanjeet graduated with an MBBS from Delhi University. Arriving in Britain, she enrolled at the University of Reading for a certificate in teaching.

Sharanjeet Shan

Her career in education began at Brudenell Secondary School in Buckinghamshire teaching mathematics and science. After moving on to Radcliffe School, where she taught for two years, she was appointed examiner for 'O' level mathematics and biology until 1985. In 1978, Sharanjeet took a place with Home School Link/Early Years for one year and then Wolverton College of F.E. for another year.

In 1981, Sharanjeet took two years out to study for RSA certificate of TESL (Teaching English as Second Language) at Bedford College. After completion, she joined Stantonbury Youth Campus as a part-time youth worker, setting up provision for black youth, environment projects, organising community arts festivals and welfare rights for Asian women and girls. In addition, she was studying Developing Mathematical Thinking, Mathematics and Science with the Open University. After completing her studies and building up her experience in working with youth, she became an advisory teacher, responsible for curriculum development and material production in mathematics, science, geography and environment education, as well as conducting workshops nationally on critical perspectives in mathematics and science.

At this time, Sharanjeet also published her first book "In my own name".

In 1988, she became head of training development at a teachers' centre in Birmingham, where she was responsible for the 'enhancement of development' project, covering 22 primary schools for an eight month period, moving on to the post of Primary Science Advisory Teacher.

Recognised for her work on training and development, she was appointed General Adviser of National Curriculum Assesment in Sandwell from 1990 until 1995. In 1993, Sharanjeet trained as an inspector with the Office For Standards in Education and was appointed a General Adviser.

Involved in launching the Association of Mathematics Educators of South Africa in 1993, she was invited to deliver a teacher-leadership course in 1994, following the success of which she was appointed Executive Director for a Mathematics Centre for Primary Teachers in Johannesburg, South Africa, where she now resides with her husband and their youngest son.

In addition to her varied teaching and training roles over the years, Sharanjeet has spoken at many seminars, launched International Woman Day in Leicester and Coventry, participated in debates on BBC, Radio West, Midlands and Radio Leicester, Central Television and Womans Hour, advised on race and gender perspectives in science, mathematics and English, contributed to NCC Guidance on Environmental Education and Equal Opportunities, written papers on issues concerning racism, mathematics, science, the Chipko Movement in India and Monolingual Teachers Assessing Emergent Bilinguals, co-published her Second book, "Multiple Factors: Classroom Mathematics for Equality and Justice", with Peter Bailey in 1991 and is hot on the trail of having her third book, "The Culture of Hope & Anger", published.

# Anita Sharma

Anita Sharma was born in 1952 in Delhi and came to England in 1978.

As a qualified General Practitioner, Anita established her practice from scratch single-handedly in Oldham. She is a trainer in Family Planning and provides Family Planning services in the Rochdale area. Being fluent in Hindi and Punjabi, she sees a majority of Asian women with language problems.

Recently she has become involved in providing education on family planning methods to young people between the ages of

11 and 13 years.

Anita is actively involved with Rochdale Indian Association, being elected as Vice-President – the first ever women to hold this position.

Anita also jointly owns a Nursing Home in the area, which provides good quality care to 24 residents at a time.

Anita married Ravi Kant, the have two children (18 year old daughter and a 13 year old son), she enjoys reading, music and knitting.

# Nita Sharma

Nita Sharma founded her consultancy practice, Sharma Associates, to pursue her vision of bringing together culture, diversity, gender, race and religion.

Nita Sharma

Nita has a BSc Hons and an MA. She has worked as a manager in Local Authorities and as an Equality Manager at the BBC.

These high-profile positions gave her much needed practical experience in management and highlighted the needs of facilitating learning and self-discovery for the mutual benefit of individuals and organisations within management.

Nita's values are about creating situations which support and enhance the diversity issues of human potential. Charged with the enthusiasm to fill this niche, she opened her consultancy practice in 1994. The organisation is committed to influencing people's lives by creating energies which combine and integrate the needs and goals of individuals and organisations and she has developed and marketed a successful programme targeting "Women in Business" for the Training Enterprise Council.

Nita is catalyst for people's hearts and minds to come together in harmony and priorities by building diverse, effective and flexible teams.

# Seema Sharma

Seema Sharma was born in Zambia in 1967 and came to England in the summer of 1983, where she continued her education. Attaining her degree in Dental Surgery at Guy's Dental Hospital in 1989 and her Licentiate the following year, she worked as an associate dentist gaining further knowledge and experience.

Seema moved to the Docklands as her parents had purchased a flat in the area, although they still lived in Zambia at that time. She noticed that the area had poor provision of dental services, so in 1991 she looked into the possibility of setting up a new dental practice, which would provide the most comprehensive possible dental care of the highest quality, at affordable prices.

With a lot of help and advice from her father and brother, both chartered accountants, and moral support and encouragement from her mother, a primary school teacher, Seema rented an empty 1,000 square foot office unit, for an initial period of three years, installed a single surgery and aptly named it the Docklands Dental and Complementary Health Centre.

Seema Sharma

Today the centre has over 6,000 patients, five part-time associate dentists, a hygienist, and six supporting staff. The incorporation of a complementary health centre provides much needed chiropody, osteopathy and physiotherapy services.

Firmly believing that there is a need for female entrepreneurship, Seema feels that women and girls need to know that they can successfully run their own business. She was runner up for the 'Working Women Mean Business' award held by Options Magazine and Mercury Communications in 1995 and was presented with a trophy by Richard Branson. An article on Seema's winning formula was featured in the Evening Standard, Dentistry Monthly, Options magazine and a number of other publications.

She is a member of the Asian Odontological Group and a committee member of Women in Docklands.

Together with her husband Sanjay, a cardiologist, Seema is now fitting out a combined centre for cardiology, dental and complementary health care in new premises, scheduled to open in 1998.

# Sabiha Sheriff

Born into a middle class family in London in 1966, Sabiha Sheriff was educated at the local primary and comprehensive schools.

At the age of 5, Sabiha was attending marches and rallies in Trafalgar Square, watching her father give speeches to thousands of people on the treatment of West Pakistani prisoners-of-war (one of whom was her uncle) during the 1971 Bangladesh war of independence. Although too young to fully comprehend the atrocities her father was fighting against, her brief encounter with human rights violation was to shape the rest of her life. The campaigning, however, took its toll on her father and, at the age of 43, he had what was to be his first heart attack. The war ended shortly after that and, with it, his campaign.

In 1979, Sabiha's family bought the archetypal corner shop. It was hard work for her parents, opening 10 hours a day, seven days a week, 365 days of the year, but Sabiha's father was the happiest he had ever been. Sabiha also enjoyed working in the shop, especially meeting and talking to lots of different people. It was during this time that Sabiha embarked on her first campaign at the age of 14. In just one weekend, in between serving customers, Sabiha managed to gather over 200 signatures for a petition against a local school which had suspended a Sikh boy because he had refused to cut his hair. The campaign was a success and the boy was allowed back to school wearing his turban.

When Sabiha was 16, her mother and sister went on holiday leaving her to look after her father, brother, the house as well as the day to day running of the business. During this time, Sabiha and her father developed a mutual respect for one another and became so close they would even talk about setting up in business together as soon as Sabiha finished her education. Sadly, he died of a second heart attack the following year.

Sabiha Sheriff

For two years after her father's death, Sabiha tried to continue with her studies but found it difficult as most of her spare time was spent working in the shop. After failing her 'A' levels at the age of 19, she decided to put her studies on hold and help run the business full-time with her mother. The responsibility of managing the business and coping with her father's death meant Sabiha had to grow up very quickly.

Finally in 1989, the shop was sold and, after a number of temporary jobs, Sabiha decided it was time to restart her education. Having completed a year on an access course, she embarked on a four year degree in Business Information and Technology at Kingston University. Upon completion, she worked for a local radio station in the evenings as a news broadcaster. This experience confirmed that journalism was the career she wanted to pursue. Undaunted by her lack of journalistic qualifications and experience, she was confident she would make an excellent journalist and resigned her job as a market researcher after just six months. Fortunately, within one month of resigning, she was recruited as a junior reporter with Sunrise Radio and, 17 months later, made Newsroom Editor.

Sabiha still wishes she and her father had been able to set up in a business together. However, she feels that by reporting on the ongoing issues of human rights violations in the Indian subcontinent, she continues to keep her father's memory and his fight for the better treatment of those who are less fortunate alive.

# Chand Sherma

Chand Sherma is a writer, producer, broadcaster, actress and court interpreter. Who insists her "one aim in life is to fight social injustice and discrimination, be it on the grounds of gender, race or class."

She was born in Quetta, capital of the Pakistan state of Baluchistan in 1952, to a privileged background. Later the family moved to Chandigarh, India. After school, her father refused to pay for her university education. But she persevered, took a job and secured an MA in Political Science.

Chand Sherma

At a very young age, she became aware of gender discrimination both in her own family and in society at large.

When she was four months pregnant with her son, her husband abandoned her, leaving her stranded in a friend's house with no money or resources.

Her brother was a consultant in Kent and she travelled overland to England, when seven and a half months pregnant, spending thirteen hours a day for a week on a bus from Tehran to Munich. She has practically no money but, people along the way helped her. On arrival in Britain her brother refused to help her, but an English family provided her with shelter for fifteen months.

Chand always wanted to act but was only ever offered stereotypical roles. Eventually, her frustrations led her to found her own theatre company. Navrang Theatre (New Vision) in 1992.

# Hannana Siddiqui

Educated to degree level, Hannana siddiqui is currently working as a Community/caseworker and Counsellor Black Sisters.

The organisation was established in 1979 to address the need (Asian, African, and Caribbean) women, although in practice assistance is given to all women who seek it regardless of racial and cultural background. The majority of the women who come to the centre are of Asian origin, reflecting the ethnic make up of the local population. Most women seel help to escape domestic violence and other forms of abuse, including force arranged marriages. Homelessness, welfare benefits and immigration are among the other prominent issues taken up by the Black Sisters. The organisation successfully campaigned for the release of Kiranjit Ahluwalia, who killed her husband after suffering 10 years of violence at his hands and to reform the homicide law particularly regarding Provocation and self-defence.

Over the years, the organisation has developed a nationally recognised expertise on the needs of Asian women.

In 1994, Southall Black Sisters won Liberty's Martin Ennals' Award for Civil Liberties for their "outstanding contribution towards the furtherance of civil liberties and human rights in the UK" and, in 1994 they secured the Advice 2000 "Challenge Award" in recognition of efforts to gain justice".

This illustrates something of the work Hannana has been involved in during her nine years at Southall Black Sisters. Prior to this, she was co-ordinator for a London-Wide Asian Women's organisation and worked on race relations housing with local authority as well as the voluntary sector.

Hannanna is also a founding member of Women Against Fundamentalism.

# Nahid Siddiqui

Born in Lahore in 1957, award winning Kathak dancer, Nahid Siddiqui, came to England in 1979 after her TV series was banned in Pakistan because it was perceived as immoral and a threat to the younger generation.

At the age of 14, she became aware of her attraction to dance and started formal lessons. From the first time she danced, she felt her body in a different way and became aware of it as a spiritual object.

Before she encountered dance, living was found to be a burden and she felt a need to have total harmony with the spirit. As a woman she respects her feelings of finding dance beautiful and asserts that every woman should have respect for themselves and their beliefs without having to explain their existence.

Nahid Siddiqui

For her, proving this has been a life-threatening experience because, under martial law, dancing became immoral and she was made to feel an outcast. Her environment was surrounded by ignorance, hate, intimidation and fear but through sheer determination and belief in herself, she fled Pakistan at the age of 22 in a bid to survive and be accepted for who she is. Despite this negative experience, her longing for home has not diminished.

She feels alive when she dances because it lifts her spirits and for her it is as natural as breathing.

# Surjit Kaur Sidhu

A life long socialist, Surjit Kaur Sidhu was born in Punjab in 1934. From an early age she was aware of the position of Asian girls within the culture. The process of thought and feelings led her to be very sensitive and creative and she has managed to weave all these diverse threads of experience together into her poems and writings. She graduated with a BA and marriage followed. Her husband Pretam Singh who was also a socialist, meant they shared a set of cultural, political and social values and understanding of the world.

Surjit Kaur Sidhu

Moving and settling in London was an uprooting experience. She managed to juggle her time successfully to train as a nurse and bringing up three boys. She has instilled in her children, a sense of duty and responsibility. She believes in a much gentler holistic kind of education which stretches the spiritual self rather than concentrating purely on prescribed cultural and religious values.

Her own experience reflects on the fact that women struggle for a fair part of their lives to have a positive sense of self. Battling for justice for all, she constantly discovers reserves of strength deep within herself.

# Gurminder Kaur Sikand

Gurminder Kaur Sikand, an artist whose work combines the figures and themes of Hindu mythology with the iconography of other cultures, was born in Jamshedpur, India in 1960.

Gurminder began her art training in Cardiff where she completed a Foundation Course in Art & Design in 1983. She then went on to graduate with a BA Hons in Fine Art Painting at Birmingham Polytechnic.

The fusions of Gurminder's work reflect on her experiences of the family's move from India to Britain at the age of 10 and draws upon her inspiration from her Asian background and Western surroundings. One of her greatest influences has been the women painters of the Mithila region of South India, whose techniques she uses in combination with those she has been taught in Britain. Her aim is to draw the two cultures together and she combines them with her thoughts ideas and life experiences. Much of her symbolism relates to birth, death, and rebirth. One of her favourite creations is "Nathaniel Rajinder", born in 1995.

Since graduating, Gurminder has exhibited widely. Her work has been presented in Black and Asian exhibitions such as "Three Asian Artists", Commonwealth Institute in 1985, "Black Art: Plotting the Course", Oldham Art Gallery, 1989; mixed exhibitions such as "Myth, Dreaming and Fable" at the Angel Row Gallery, Nottingham in 1992; and solo exhibitions, the first being the Artist Showcase, Nottingham Castle Museum, 1985 and her most recent "Wonderings in Paint" at Nottingham University Art Gallery, 1994, where she was the Artist in Residence from 1993-1994.

Her paintings featured in catalogues such as "The Circular Dance" and "Black Art: Plotting the Course". The accessibility of her work is plainly revealed when one sees the range of organisations and private collectors which have purchased her work including, The Arts Council, Sheffield's Graves Gallery, and Nottingham Castle, as well as numerous schools such as Grove Junior School, Birmingham, The Leicestershire Collection for Schools and Colleges.

Gurminder's commitment to sharing her talent and knowledge is apparent. She has been involved in many residencies and workshops, given talks in schools, galleries and community centres where she has worked with people from a range of cultural backgrounds, abilities and age groups. She feels it is important to widen the understanding and appreciation of art.

Joanna Wright, Director of Nottingham University Art Gallery, sums up Gurminder's perceptions: "Gurminder muses on the Hindu notion that life is an illusion and also on the metaphor of life as a dance".

# Ajeet Harbans Singh

Ajeet Harbans Singh, affectionately known as Parsan, is a Justice of the Peace for Middlesex Petty Sessions Area.

Born in Tanzania in 1932, the youngest of four children, Ajeet had a happy and cosmopolitan upbringing and whilst still very young the family moved to Calcutta. Her father, an Indian Police Officer, wanted his children to have a good all round education. As well as attending the best Urdu school in the area, Ajeet was taught to play the sitar, sing and shoot a rifle. She graduated with a BA degree and then went on to read Law at Calcutta University.

Marriage followed university, to Harbans Singh, a member of the Indian Diplomatic Service from a very distinguished family, who was home on leave from London. Her first meeting with her future husband was on their wedding day, but she confirms today that her marriage is a real partnership.

Arriving in Britain in 1953 with her husband, Ajeet was lucky to find work initially at her husband's office. With the birth of their first child, a girl, there was much media coverage as hers was the first Sikh Naming Ceremony to be covered by the press. While her daughter was young, Ajeet continued with her social and cultural work, organising and performing at functions for audiences who were homesick for their native culture. In 1959 Ajeet had the honour of performing for the Queen Mother at Marlborough House. Attaining a second place in a beauty contest in Acton, west London, she went on to small parts in films such as "Doctor in the House"

Ajeet became the first female Indian Education Welfare Officer. In addition to working as a voluntary probation officer, she was appointed to the Special Health Authority for hospitals including Hammersmith and Queen Charlotte's and was involved with the Women's Council of Great Britain and the Indian High Commission Ladies Association.

She became a Magistrate for Middlesex Petty Sessions Area in 1985.

# Amrit and Rabindra Kaur Singh

Amrit and Rabindra Kaur Singh

"Our works emphasise all that is positive and valuable about Asian culture", claim artists Amrit and Rabindra Kaur Singh. These sisters from Wirral, Merseyside, whose identity as twins rings out loud in all their endeavours, have dedicated themselves to reviving and developing the tradition of Indian miniature painting and have established themselves as pioneers in a unique area of research – Sikh religious art.

Born in London in 1966, they attended a Catholic Convent School and grew up in an area isolated from the wider Asian community. Consequently, in their early childhood they knew very little of their Asian roots. A visit to India when they were 14 proved to be a critical turning point. They felt a spontaneous affiliation with every aspect of Indian culture – history, dress, arts, philosophy and values – which was to guide the course of their future career. From then on they made a conscious effort to assert their Asian identity and sense of pride in Indian culture.

In 1985, they enrolled for a BA Hons. degree in Comparative Religion, Ecclesiastical History and 20th Century Art. During this time, they developed a form of art which in style and content sought to challenge preconceived ideas of Western superiority. Most importantly, it also attempted to counter the generally negative stereotypes of 'Asian-ness' propagated by the mass media. However, their controversial work led to a downgraded mark in their degree. They challenged the university and after four years of sustained effort, won the appeal to have their degrees upgraded and set a precedent for future such cases.

In 1994, they were both elected members of the Manchester Academy of Fine Arts. Promoting themselves under the name Twin Studio, their commitment and work have won recognition and attracted media attention including television and radio, and articles in The Guardian, The Artist, Calcutta Telegraph and India Today. They have exhibited their art in solo and group shows around Britain over the last ten years, and have paintings in both private and public galleries throughout the world. The most recent acquisition was by the Liverpool Museum's Social History Department – a painting on football in Liverpool in the Indian miniature style. Similarly, they have received commission requests from the Glasgow St. Mungo Museum of Religious Life and Art and Cartwright Hall Bradford City Gallery as well as from private individuals.

In their current postgraduate research on Sikh Religious Art at Manchester University, they hope to cover the development of Sikh art from its earliest representations in illustrated manuscripts of the 17th-19th Centuries, to its present and most popular and universal format of mass produced imagery. As part of these studies they won a grant from the Indian National Trust for Art and Cultural Heritage in 1990-91, to carry out field research in India for one year.

They were nominees for 'Best New Talent' in the 1997 'Merseyside Arts and Entertainment Awards' and have been selected to represent Liverpool in a multi-media exhibition that will tour internationally.

Prime among their forthcoming ventures are invitations to participate in staging an exhibition on the theme "Indian Independence" in 1997.

# Rani Singh

Rani Singh was born in London in 1959 and studied at Haberdashers' Askes' Girls' School in Elstree. With persistence to carve herself a career, she gained a BA in Performance Arts from Middlesex University, where she specialised in Indian Classical Literature, beginning her love for directing and writing.

Rani Singh

After graduating, Rani founded Singh Theatre, where she remains as Artistic Director. The only South Asian Theatre Company in Great Britain exclusively using Indian masks and puppets to bring culture from the Sub-Continent to Western audiences, the group has toured extensively since 1982, participating in international festivals, visiting remote corners of the British Isles and playing in a variety of venues from theatres to schools. Without fail, every Autumn for the last 13 years, Singh Theatre has performed the Ramayana in season at the Commonwealth Institute in London.

In 1987, Christian Aid sent the company to research and train in India, exploring aspects of social justice and advocacy on the Sub-Continent.

A collaborative residency at the Scottish Mank and Puppet Centre, in 1993, they produced Panchatantra in shadow puppet form and premiered a dramatisation from the Arabian Nights for Manchester City of Drama in 1994.

Through the company, Rani has presented a series of films for the United Nations and for three years starred as Sufia Karim in BBC's Eastenders.

She increasingly participates in inter-cultural collaborations as she works to strengthen links between South Asia and the international community and. Since 1982, has written for radio, television and print media, including a trilogy based on the 1947 War of Partition, a BBC radio play The King of the Golden Dear, a report for BBC TV Women of South Asia and four books - The Indian Story Book, Stories From the Sikh World, The Amazing Adventures of Hanuman and The Four Friends. In 1993, she trained to be a BBC Radio Drama Director and brought the Ramayana story to the department. Involved in features and current affairs, she wrote and presented a radio documentary about the Ramayana.

A member of the Indian Journalists Association and the Society of Authors, from 1985 to 1991 she was an executive member of the UK Christian Aid Development Education Committee; from 1990 to 1992 an the executive member of the Calouste-Gulbenkian Enquiry Committee which produced the book On the Brink of Belonging and a Judge for the Commission for Racial Equality's annual Race in the Media Awards since 1992.

In 1997, she was Judge for the Sony Awards and produced a specially commissioned set of short stories from premier Indian writers for Radio 4. She also produces and presents programmes for other networks.

# Sukhvinder Kaur Stubbs

Sukhvinder Kaur Stubbs

Born in the district of Jullunder at the time of Divali, Sukhvinder Stubbs arrived in Britain with her parents, who migrated with a work voucher. Bright and intelligent, she had no difficulty grasping the English language even though she was late starting school. Although she was brought up and educated in Britain, she has never quite felt she belonged here, even since acquiring a British passport.

Sukhvinder went on to Oxford University where she won the top University prize in 1984 and met David Stubbs, whom she married shortly after graduation at a Sikh ceremony. Joining British Telecom as a management trainee, Sukhvinder also gained experience teaching at a Further Education college. Throughout her life she has been actively involved with the voluntary sector. In the late 1980s she started to work professionally with voluntary organisations. This included third world agencies, welfare of prisoners, educational trusts and community development. She has also worked as a Civil Servant in the Home Office and Department of Environment quangos.

Her contributions and achievements include serving as a Board Director for the Greenwich and Dockland International Festival in 1993, appointed by the Secretary of State to the Board of the Black Country Development Corporation in 1993, elected Non Executive Director for Queen Mary's NHS Trust in Sidcup in 1995 and Fellow of the Royal Society of Arts.

Appointed as Chief Executive with Runnymead Trust, an independent think tank and social policy agency on race relations and cultural diversity, she feels through her work she is given the opportunity to make a real difference to the lives of ethnic minorities in Britain. This for Sukhvinder has fulfilled a long standing desire to put something back into her community in a way that she is unable to do directly for her family.

# Asma Hatim Suterwalla

Asma Hatim Suterwalla was born in 1945 in Bombay, where she studied up to Inter Arts at Jai Hind College, Bombay. Her reminiscences of childhood are of fun and freedom to develop in a close knit society.

In 1957, Asma went to Uganda and Kenya with her mother in anticipation of settling down in Uganda. After four months, her mother's patriotic longing for India became overwhelming and they decided to return to Bombay.

In 1964, Asma married Hatim a businessman and they came to Britain for permanent settlement, joining her husband's family. Initially she found it very hard to adapt to the ways of life in England but the patriotic feelings for the adopted country developed with the guidance and security of a respectful father-in-law who was a wise and successful businessman. She settled into the joint family with the positive support of her husband. She progressed smoothly and began to find the experience fulfilling and rewarding.

Between 1965 and 1969, Asma manned the family's handicraft stand at the Ideal Home Exhibition at Olympia. She trained and began teaching English as a volunteer at an Adult Literary centre. The number of white people who were unable to read and write made her aware of the level of illiteracy in the indigenous population

Asma went on to study for three years to attain her City & Guilds Fashion Designing Certificates, and started teaching dressmaking in community centres. Musically talented Asma is learning to play harmonium and vocal training from her music tutor Pandit Vishwa Prakash. She sung a song in Praise of Allah which has been played on Sunrise radio for the last two years during the month of Ramadan, the lyrics and music for this song was composed by her music tutor.

She finds travel extremely fascinating and has travelled extensively. She also takes a keen interest in cultural activities, music, ghazals. and keeps fit by practising yoga and aerobics.

# Meera Syal

Meera Syal, an actress and writer whose passion is to be 'a proper Indian', feels that somebody has got to take a cool, reflective look at Asians in Britain today.

Born in Wolverhampton in 1963, duty and desire formed the basic tension of Meera's life - duty to her parents and culture and desire to find out who she really was.

She grew up during the years when Enoch Powell made speeches and the Southall riots took place. Her parents kept a certain insularity but this didn't apply to her generation. They were born here. They didn't have another world they could carry around in their heads. They had to compete. They had to take on a lot of the battles that their parents couldn't or wouldn't engage in and they had to redefine the image their parents had given of Indians as ethereal, exotic people, clannish and never quite involved.

Meera Syal

At the age of nine, Meera started to put on weight until then she was a dainty little thing. She ate out of misery; the frustration that she wanted to do something creative but didn't think it would be possible. Her parents wanted her to study science or become a medic but at the age of 15, sensed her unhappiness and accepted her decision not become a doctor. Gaining three A's in English, French and Spanish, she went to Manchester University to read English and Drama.

She was doing what she wanted to do but, now it was a different kind of frustration: she was gauche. Being fat meant she had two choices - sad soul or class clown. She chose to be the clown, everybody's friend and nobody's lover because taking a lover meant she would be a 'bad' Indian woman, not a 'proper' Indian woman. And she couldn't risk that. So being fat became a way of being Indian and protected her from that old fear, rejection - releasing her from the choices she had to make. It took her a long time to work it out. She started to be clear about who she was when she began visiting India because she saw that India was changing too.

Not picked for the good parts in University stage productions, she wrote her own play, One of Us, which won the National Student Drama Award. A director of the Royal Court Theatre saw her in it and offered the chance of an Equity card. She threw in the idea of reading an MA in Drama and Psychotherapy, started to act and, like a miracle, started to get thin.

After seven years of acting in new plays, she got a call from the BBC who wanted an Asian woman to co-write a script. Not wanting to write the usual cliches, she wrote My Sister Wife, a three part television serial. Writing is lonely and hard but the pleasure of writing as an Asian woman is the pleasure of exploding stereotypes.

Her next film, Bhaji On The Beach, aroused considerable criticism from Asian community leaders because she was washing dirty linen in public. But she wanted to show that Indian women are simply human, not Gods.

It was out of this sensation of flux that Meera wrote Anita & Me, a novel that looks nostalgically back to warmer days but pragmatically forward - not necessarily to better times, just different.

# Rekha Tandon

Dr Rekha Tandon was born in Poona, India. The eldest of five sisters, she was educated in various cities around the country including Aligarh, Bareilly, Lucknow and Kanpur. She qualified with her medical degree from the GSVM Medical College in Kanpur in 1971, and completed a postgraduate diploma in Paediatric Medicine in 1973.

In 1973, she married Dr Pradip Tandon, also a graduate of GSVM medical school, Kanpur. The couple came to the Britain in 1976, where they completed their hospital training before settling down as General Practitioners in a joint General Practice in Wallasey, Wirral.

Since completing her degree, she has developed interests in various aspects of medicine such as hypnotherapy and homeopathy, largely influenced by her grandfather's work as a homeopathic doctor. In 1993, she was deeply moved when one of her patients developed AIDS and this prompted her to take a postgraduate diploma in genito-urinary medicine from Liverpool University in order to learn more about the treatment and care of such patients.

As a devoted mother, Rekha has brought up her two daughters to appreciate both the arts and the sciences. She has passed on her knowledge and love of classical Indian dance while also encouraging them to become high achievers themselves.

Rekha is involved with ActionAid with whom she sponsors a child in South India to aid his upbringing and education. She has also organised many fund-raising activities with different charities, some of which have been as a result of her involvement in the Overseas Doctors Association, of which her husband is Deputy Treasurer.

As a young girl, Rekha was extremely fortunate to hear about the personal and political life of Mahatma Gandhi from her grandfather, Mr Parsu Ram Mehrotra, who was his Private Secretary. The letters and documents her grandfather wrote on behalf of the Mahatma were handed over to the Government of India on his death in 1996 at the age of 98. Perhaps as a result of this early influence, she has become closely involved with AHINSAM, an organisation which promotes the teaching of Indian Languages which has managed to establish a Chair of Indian Language at the University of Manchester.

Rekha's main ambition now is to see more of the world and to meet Mother Theresa of Calcutta. She will be touring China and Japan in September 1997, having already travelled all over Europe and United States of America.

# Satinder Kaur Taunque

Satinder Kaur Taunque, an active socialist and Labour Party member, was born in the Punjab, India in 1943. Graduating in India, she was married in 1968 to Councillor Jagjit Singh

Satinder Kaur Taunque

Taunque, vice-chair of West Midlands County Council. She arrived in Britain in 1969 and at present is a teacher for the Birmingham Education Authority.

For many years she has focused on work with Asian women and girls. She is former chairperson of the UK Asian Women's Organisation in Birmingham and of "Roshini", a hostel for runaway girls.

Satinder writes articles and poems in English and Punjabi. She is also the General Secretary of the Punjab Cultural Centre.

Satinder is a member of Birmingham Civic Society, East Birmingham Community Health Council, a sub committee of the Independent Broadcasting Authority, the India Club, Indian Ladies Club, Asian Parents Association, Asian Teachers Association and founder member of the Executive Committee of a "Drop-In" Centre for the elderly. She won Asian Woman of the year award in 1990.

Satinder was the first Asian to introduce an Asian menus to the Solihull Health Authority.

She comes from a patriotic Sikh family. Her grandfather, Baba Kharak Singh, was a prominent Congress leader and fought for India's independence along with Mahatma Gandhi and Jawaharlal Nehru. A road, "Baba Kharak Singh Marg", was named in his honour in New Delhi.

# Damyanti Thakker

Damyanti Thakker

Damyanti Thakker was born in Blantyre, Malawi where she completed her early education. The third born only girl of six children, she asserted herself and expected to get the same treatment as her brothers.

Confident and independent, she had the same ambitions and desire for achievement as her brothers. As her brothers studied in England, it was imperative to Damyanti that she too went abroad for higher education. Her parents considered it important to impress upon their daughter the influence of the Indian culture. So came about the move to India for Damyanti. With encouragement from her family and the free will to choose, she read English Literature and Psychology at Sophia College, University of Bombay.

While at university, Damyanti was actively involved in Student Union affairs and involved in many rural development projects and she particularly remembers the month she spent at a camp on the India/Pakistan border before the Independence of Bangladesh in 1972.

Returning to Malawi after graduation, Damyanti wanted to study further for a professional qualification and was again greatly encouraged by her parents and brothers to follow that course. With her two elder brothers involved in law came the influence to choose the same route.

Arriving in England in 1975, she successfully qualified as a solicitor in 1978 and married a Bharat Chartered Accountant the same year.

Initially working part-time to devote time to her children, Damyanti set up her own practice when the children were settled in full-time education.

As well as being involved in other women's organisations and issues, her commitment to voluntary work is apparent at Harrow Women's Centre, where she provides free legal advice.

As personal well-being is also important to Damyanti, she plays tennis and works out at her local gym.

# Alka Trivedi

Alka Trivedi was born in Indore, India in 1950. After completing her postgraduate MS in 1976 Alka came to Britain the following year and has been working in Wigan since then.

In Dublin she completed her Diploma postgraduate course in 1979, going on to work in Obstetrics/Gynaecology and Family Planning Training course for a few years. Alka then decided to do General Practice which she has been doing since 1983.

She is very active in the Overseas Doctor's Association of which she is a National Executive Member and National Secretary for Women's Forum. She has attended many medical conferences in the UK, Europe, Egypt, America and India. She is very much involved in charity work collecting and donating money to hospice's, Leukaemia Research and Help the Blind a charity in India.

Alka Trivedi

She is married to Dr. Deepak Trivedi who is a General Practitioner in Wigan and is National Vice-chairman of Overseas Doctor's Association in UK Ltd.

Their two children, son Alankar and Daughter, Twinki (Anita) one focus of her life and source of a lot of joy.

She enjoys swimming, music, singing, dancing and playing table tennis.

# T. Reshmi Varma

Born in Madras, India, Reshmi Varma graduated from the University of Madras in 1960 as student of the year, winning several gold medals, certificates of merit and honours.

Arriving in Britain in 1965, she received her PhD from the University of London in 1975. Continuing her education, she was awarded by the Royal College of Obstetricians and

Gynaecologists in 1981 and was elected a member of the New York Academy of Sciences in March 1997.

T. Reshmi Varma

After appointment to St. George's Medical School, Reshmi set up the academic unit, organising teaching programmes for under and post-graduates and setting up the fertility, menopause and ultrasound services.

In addition to her work at the hospital, Reshmi is a writer, editor, lecturer and external examiner.

In April 1997, Reshmi felt obliged to resign from her position at St. George's Hospital due to the medical school closing a very well-run fertility unit, leading to the loss of eight members of staff. Constantly struggling facing many problems Rashmi feels her unit was targeted despite its success.

# Merlyn Verona Vaz

Merlyn Verona Vaz was born in 1929 and educated in Bombay, India. She taught in Aden between 1954 – 1965 before coming to England in August 1965. When she arrived she had to retrain, gaining a BEd degree in 1980, a period which she thoroughly enjoyed. After qualifying, Merlyn chose to remain in the teaching profession, in which she remained for 36 years.

Since retiring, she has taken up the post of Councillor for Leicester City Council and is active on many committees. As the only black woman on Leicester City Council, she works to 'politicise' women, especially those of Asian origin, and feels women must support each other, although they also need the support of men.

A widow for 26 years, Merlyn has three children, two daughters and a son, all of whom are solicitors, while her son Keith is also a barrister and MP from Leicester East. She has five grandchildren aged 11 months to 18 years.

# Valerie Carol Marian Vaz

Valerie Carol Marian Vaz

Valerie Carol Marian Vaz was born in Aden, Yemen in 1954. With a desire to continue further education, she arrived in England in 1965. Attaining a degree in Biochemistry at the University of London, Valerie went on to qualify as a solicitor in 1982 at the College of Law.

Beginning her legal career in 1985, she commenced work as a local government solicitor, a post she held until 1992. Wanting to add a little light relief, she presented 'Network East' on BBC Television in 1987.

Elected as a councillor for the London Borough of Ealing from 1986 to 1990, she was also a school governor during this period. Her work with local government prompted her to stand as a parliamentary candidate for the General Election in 1987.

After leaving her solicitor post within local government, Valerie and her husband founded Townsend Vaz Solicitors in 1992.

Committed to serving the community, Valerie has been the Chair of the Police Committee and Community Action Policy Group; the vice-chair of Health and Social Services Committee; a member of Housing, Environmental Services, Policy and Resources Committees and a member of Ealing District Health Authority.

A published writer, she has written on topics such as health, women and legal services for the Tribune, Asian Times, Eastern Eye and the Ealing Gazette.

# Veena Verma

Veena Verma, for whom the road to becoming a social worker has been an arduous one, was born in Budhlada, India in 1960

Veena graduated from Patiala University with a BA and a B Ed degree, she participated in numerous activities, outside University at drama clubs and youth festivals, local temples, cultural centres and wrote poetry and short stories.

After completing her education, she arrived in Britain for marriage, which unfortunately did not work out. Life became very difficult for her after separation because she was naive to the English system and had no family to support her. Struggling to survive, she realised the difficulties Asian women had to face in

Veena Verma

a male dominated white society, and fought for her identity and rights.

Realising she needed to find a means to support herself, she began working at the prominent Asian newspaper, "Des Pardes", as a journalist. Through her work Veena became aware of community issues such as racism, discrimination and oppression. These issues spurred Veena on to writing several articles which were published in national newspapers. Her first book "Mulher Dee Tiwin", a collection of stories about the plight of different women, was published in 1994 and sold very successfully.

She then joined Ealing Health Authority as a bilingual interpreter and it was here she decided that, in order to best serve her community, she needed to re-educate herself to gain British qualifications and enrolled at Brunei University to study for a Diploma in Social Work.

Since qualifying, Veena has been a social worker in the London boroughs and also enjoys doing voluntary work at Asian community and day centres.

Although dedicating most of her time to her work, Veena participates in literary seminars and writes poems and short stories. Her emphasis on the plight of women is sensitively portrayed in her Punjabi poems and short stories are being published in a book.

## Shaila Virani

Shaila Virani

Shaila Virani is an Ismaili Muslim and was born in Uganda. At the age of one her family left their home due to the Asian expulsion in 1972. She graduated from Warwick University in Economics.

With a technological revolution advancing upon us, Shaila saw the need of involving the minority community as vital. With intensive research and planning, Shaila saw that Information Technology was a power that could be used in supporting and enhancing the Asian market. Hence, at the age of 26, she has launched through this vision the Asian-Online website (www.asian.online.co.uk) to service the entire Asian community.

Asian-Online is the dream created from her aspirations that drove Shaila in her venture. The Internet website was designed to bring all Asian businesses together without exception or boundary. The website incorporates "The Brown Pages", a comprehensive directory of all UK Asian businesses and professionals. Furthermore the site also encompasses cultural services dedicated to fashion, tradition, traditional cuisine, a marriage bureau, news and sport.

Shaila Virani had undoubtedly succeeded in this unusual and challenging endeavour. With a carefully selected team of expertise, she is constantly enhancing and exploring new possibilities for the future.

## Jasbir Vohra

Committed and determined Jasbir Vohra was born in Kenya in November 1942. After completing school at 17, she arrived in Britain to study nursing and mid-wifery under the auspices of the British Council.

Although missing home, she loved and adapted to her new environment quickly. Through the British Council, summer holiday months were spent with selected families to ensure the student got an opportunity to be in a family environment. Jasbir found that although there were very few Asians in Britain at that time, people were liberated and generous, so memories of her early years in Britain remain fond ones.

Whilst studying, Jasbir used to travel to London on Sundays to a small Gurudwara in Shepherds Bush to keep in touch with the Sikh community. She met her future husband Kughi there and a few years later after their graduation, they married and moved to Queensway near Paddington. Jasbir started work with St. Mary's Hospital and her husband set up his own chartered flights company, which regularly took him to all parts of Britain, visiting Universities to sell flights to overseas students. To avoid loneliness, they joined the overseas club to meet other Asians.

Her husband's business was flourishing but at the age of 29, he suddenly became ill. Losing appetite and weight, he continued to make regular trips to keep the business going. Eventually a biopsy was carried out and cancer was diagnosed. Within 2 weeks, a major operated was performed, followed by radiotherapy. This treatment had not worked and cancer spread into his lymph glands. Over the next months, four major operations were performed, which meant Jasbir attending hospital for 16 hours each day. In order to cope with her emotions and be practical, Jasbir arranged to send her 6 month daughter to her mother-in-law in Kenya, whilst she kept her 3 year old son in London. With her internal strength, support and assistance from the family, Jasbir coped but the chartered flight business collapsed.

Once her husband fully recovered and with support from family, they purchase a small hotel, carrying out daily duties personally until enough staff were employed. The family now own The Rembrandt Hotel in London which it continues to thrive and flourish with much personal attention given by the family to it's decor and service.

Jasbir has maintained connections with the organisations she joined in her early years in Britain, particularly Women's India for which she was the Chairman from 1993 to 1995. She belongs to many other charitable and religious associations, one of which is Hemkunt Childrens Education Society, in which she is involved running a fee-free school on Friday, Saturday and Sunday. They teach languages, religion and musical instruments, as well as arranging for the children to participate in poetry and essay competitions which take place around the world.

Jasbir also belongs to medical groups who help the Asian community in times of need in various ways, one of which is translating for patients who do not speak English, and visiting patients in hospitals and in their homes who just want to talk to someone or need help advice, because of depression and loneliness.

A committed mother and grandmother, Jasbir is a practical, stable and consistent individual, who's strengths are derived from her deeply rooted spiritual beliefs.

# Tilusha Vyas

Tilusha Vyas was born in Uganda, and came to Britain in 1972.

Having a BSc in Economics, Tilusha joined the BBC's accounting department. Soon realising this was not the career for her, she moved on to BBC's Local Radio headquarters. She worked there for almost two years as a radio Producer/ Journalist, before moving on to BBC World Service, where she now works as a Researcher and Broadcaster.

In recent years she has also worked as a print journalist for Asian Age, an Indian newspaper published in India and England, and continues to write for India Today, an India current affairs magazine, and Libas International, a fashion magazine.

# Nina Wadia

Nina Wadia

Nina Wadia, an actress and comedienne ready to take on the world. Arriving in England in 1987, she pursued her love of the arts, taking up tap dancing, acting and singing as well as studying for her A levels.

Nina has worked with the BBC Radio Drama Company and appeared at the Theatre Royal, Stratford East in Tamasha's 'Women of the Dust' , 'House of the Sun', 'Romeo and Juliet' and 'D'yer Eat With Your Fingers.

Nina's film and television credits include 'Flight', 'Trying to Grow', '2.4 children' and 'Eastenders'. In 1995 she was presented with the Award for 'Greatest Achievement in Acting' by the Society for Black Arts.

Appearing in 'Natural World', a Kali Theatre production, in which Nina plays a lesbian half-Bengali half-Italian girl in love with a white girl, was a role she found challenging and a refreshing shift from playing the 'good Indian girl'.

Currently working on Radio 4's 'Masala FM', Nina is soon to be on television's 'Goodness Gracious Me'.

# Sunita Wallia

Sunita Wallia was born in India in 1959. Upon completing her BSc in biology and chemistry, her parents had planned for her marriage and, to escape this, Sunita came to Britain for two months and took a chance of applying for further education at Strathclyde University, where she obtained an MSc in applied microbiology in 1981.

Finally succumbing to her parents' wishes, Sunita married in 1982. Offered many jobs as a microbiologist outside of Glasgow she was unable to accept them due to 'married life restrictions'. During the following years she settled down in her new environment and observed changes in the eating behaviour of the two cultures and Asians here and back home. Prompted by her findings to do study Dietetics, she completed her postgraduate diploma in Applied Nutrition and Dietetics in 1988.

Sunita was immediately offered the post of senior dietician through which she was involved in research activities on dietary changes among South Asians and an Asian health Survey in Glasgow.

In 1993, Sunita's biggest achievement was to become the mother of twins. She returned to work when the twins were six months old, specialising as a mental health dietitian with particular interest in nutritional counselling of patients with eating disorders, taking groups sessions of alcohol rehabilitation clients.

Sunita Wallia

In 1996, Sunita took up the first-ever post of Ethnic Minorities Dietitian in Scotland, to initiate a culturally sensitive nutritional service to the ethnic minorities in Glasgow.

This post has allowed her to do some small exploratory surveys to make future recommendations. She undertook two remits:

Ethnic Minority Organisations and specific therapeutic dietary advise for disease states, patients referred from several GP practices, health centres, hospital consultants etc.

In addition to this, Sunita also undertakes part-time locum posts in hospital or community settings.

# Perween Warsi

Perween Warsi, born in India in 1956, is a successful businesswoman managing her own ethnic food company S&A Foods.

A psychology graduate, Perween arrived in Britain with her husband Tahib, a doctor, in 1975. Perween' s career in the food industry had humble beginnings in her small kitchen in Derybshire. Frustrated by the quality of Indian food in supermarkets and restaurants she decided to take matters into her own hands.

Perween Warsi

With the full support of her family, her husband and two sons, an extremely important factor for Perween, she set up S&A Foods (the initials of her two sons names) in 1986. She began by making finger foods for local restaurants and it wasn't long before there was a rapid increase in demand for her products from half a dozen of one item, to several hundred of five items per week. Perween's next step was to go nationwide and place her products in national supermarkets and, in 1987, after beating fierce competition, her company won the business to supply food to ASDA and Safeway. Through her determination and insistence for her products to be of the highest quality, S&A Foods has enjoyed a meteoric rise. Its first purpose-built factory was built in 1988 and the second was opened in 1996 by the then Deputy Prime Minister, Michael Heseltine. The company has now reached a position where it has over 400 employees and a turnover of over £30 million.

Both Perween and her company have been showered with awards and honours since 1986. S&A Foods has won awards such as British Quality Food & Drink Awards, 1994, and again in 1996, Top 100 Best Performing Companies (privately owned) UK, ranked fifth, 1994, and the silver prize at the ADAS/Sunday Telegraph Food & Drink Awards 1995, 3i Award for Manufacturers as well as many others.

Perween has herself been bestowed with a multitude of prizes including winner of the Midlands Business Woman of the Year Award 1994, runner-up in the Veuve Cliquot Business Woman of the Year, 1994 and winner of the RADAR People of the Year Awards 1995. In 1997 came the most glittering and worthy honour when Perween was awarded the MBE for her work in the food service industry. As the UK winner of the Women Entrepreneurs of the World Awards 1997, she will be appearing as a finalist at the Awards Ceremony in Los Angeles later this year.

Perween's business philosophy embodies the ideals of innovation and novelty. In constant pursuit of these ideals she travels widely researching new dishes. In 1996 she began her collaboration with Chinese celebrity chef Ken Hom to launch the new Oriental range. Perween leads with enthusiasm and is a strong believer in employee empowerment and rewarding her staff for their efforts.

"I love what I do and want to keep running the company for as long as I can," says Perween. With her excellent track record, there is no fear of anything but success in the future.

# Kulwant Wasu

Born in Lyallpur (now Pakistan), Kulwant Wasu was educated in different schools, including convents in Punjab, as a result of her doctor father's work. Inspired to work hard, the children were always reminded that 'impossible' was spelt I (A)M POSSIBLE, which is something that Kulwant still remembers.

Whilst studying for her first degree, she was actively involved in debates, drama, singing, dancing and writing articles for magazines. She was the editor of the magazines at the various colleges that she attended. As a result of winning a literary competition, she was invited to broadcast her essay on the Women's Programme on All-India Radio, which she accepted.

After completion of her first degree, she studied for her Bachelor of Training (BT) at Khalsa College, Amritsar. In 1955 she married an advocate husband and had three children, all of whom are now successful professionals in this country. Following her post graduate studies (MA), she started her teaching career in 1964 as a lecturer and Head of the History department.

In 1967, Kulwant and her family planned a move to Chandigarh but as double graduates, they were granted employment vouchers for England and instead found themselves in Kent.

Soon after arriving, she became involved in many community-based organisations to raise awareness of the Asian way of life. She co-founded the CRC (Community Relation Council) in Gravesend, which was considered to be a model town of racial harmony. She had a key position on the Social Sub-Committee and organised special events, displays on Asian culture, annual dinners and fund-raising activities for charity in the Mayor's Parlour.

Kulwant Wasu

After an initial period working in a Secondary School, she taught in primary schools with various posts of responsibility.

In 1977, she was approached to introduce Asian Cookery Classes at the North-West Kent College of Technology in the evenings, which she initially undertook on a trial basis, but demand was such that she taught this course for many years. Teaching Asian Cookery served as a useful platform for enhancing students' understanding and appreciation of Asian culture.

Kulwant then became involved in Inter-Faith meetings, which attracted people from different cultures and communities. As she shared the experiences and concerns, she analysed the needs of different ethnic minorities. It was felt that second generation children were becoming more and more alienated from their mainly non-English speaking parents, roots, culture and language, so along with two more people, she was involved in the establishment of Mother Tongue Teaching in North-West College of Technology and, after long perseverance, MTT was recognised and given a status of a modern language at 'O' level and later on at 'A' level.

In 1984, she was appointed Advisory Teacher for multicultural education, the curriculum development team and the language support service. She was also involved in the introduction of performances of Punjabi folk dances in Kent primary schools and for the first time gidha and bhangra dance performances were performed on a primary school stage in front of the local civic dignitaries along with Asian parents.

In 1989, she was promoted to County Advisory Teacher (Kent) for Multicultural Education. Her main brief was to raise awareness of the pluralistic society amongst Kent schoolteachers and Head Teachers by organising and presenting INSETs (In-Service Teacher Training) courses, conferences and seminars and arranging project work at various venues in Kent such as Eversley College, Folkestone and Christ Church College, Canterbury. Typical themes were Bilingualism, Equal Opportunities, Sikhism, Early Years and Multicultural

Education Permeates the Curriculum.

Kulwant is also author and co-author of various books included Bilingual Nursery Rhymes, Learning Is Fun Part 1, Getting Started in Schools Part II, Multicultured in Primary Schools, Units of Study for Punjabi 'O' Level and various booklets for teachers.

# Priya Wickramasinghe

Priya Wickramasinghe

Nelum Priyadarshini Wickramasinghe (known to her friends as Priya) was born in Colombo, Sri Lanka in 1945. Her mother was a head teacher and her father a lawyer. From an early age she had an ardent interest in food and cookery. She used to watch proceedings in the kitchen, take notes and compile recipe notebooks, an activity that led eventually to cookery writing on a bigger scale.

After spending two terms at Ceylon University studying law, Nelum married Chandra Wickramasinghe, an astronomer, in 1966 and shortly afterwards they arrived in Britain. The first seven years were spent in Cambridge, followed by a move to Cardiff University. She has travelled extensively in USA, Canada, Japan, Jamaica, India and Europe.

Priya attained several qualifications, including Diploma's in Pianoforte and (Teaching English as a Foreign Language) TEFL certificate in Further Education and Japanese. While playing her role as mother of three children, and hostess, she pursued her long standing passion for cooking, becoming a cookery demonstrator and writer publishing two books "Spicy and Delicious" and "The Oriental Cookbook" both of which were well reviewed and went in to mass paperback editions. Her latest book "Leith's book of Indian and Sri Lankan Cooking".

Priya has made several appearances on TV and has also taken part in radio programmes. Since the early 1980s, she has been a Guest Lecturer in Indian cooking at the Leith's School of Food and Wine in London. In 1993, Priya won the Cordon Bleu Independent Cookery Competition held in London. Her prize included a gastronomic tour to Paris.

Apart from her role as a gourmet cook and writer, Priya now works as a part-time teacher in the County of South Glamorgan.

# Amrit Wilson

Amrit Wilson was born in Calcutta, India in January 1941 and graduated with a BSc. She arrived in Britain in 1961 and, after familiarising and settling down, began to carve her career as a writer and lecturer.

She has spent the last 25 years tirelessly organising to fight women's oppression, particularly the oppression of South African women in Britain. She has also attempted to analyse the nature of this oppression and has written extensively in this context. Her publications include three books and a play which was produced by The Spinx Theatre Company and she has written many articles for journals and newspapers.

Amrit is a founder member of the South Africa Solidarity Group, which links up the South Asian experience in Britain with the democratic and revolutionary struggle in the various Asian countries of origin, and also participates in workshops on these issues.

# Kulsum Winship

Kulsum Winship

Kulsum Winship's early determination to be independent and contribute to society led her to read medicine, specialising in acute and community paediatrics. Born in Kenya in 1930, she was educated in varied environments in Kenya, Switzerland, Tanzania, India and finally the UK, studying science subjects not traditionally taught in girls' schools abroad then.

Joining the Department of Health, where she was one of the first Asian women appointed to a senior post in central government in the UK, she was part of a government team that developed policies for the management of disabled and abused children and intensive care of the new-born. Kulsum's move after some years from the division of child health to the division for regulating medicines led her into a completely new and interesting field of healthcare. She reviewed the use of medicines containing oestrogens, metals and herbal substances followed by regulatory control of their use. She has had articles published on the toxicity of oestrogens, metals used in medicines and the use of comfrey in medicines and foods.

Kulsum has been a member of a local Community Health Council and Steering Group on Ethnic Health, a non-executive director of an NHS Hospital Trust, in which she chairs the Ethnic Monitoring and Implementation Group, and is also a school governor for a school for students with severe learning disabilities.

She joined Breast Cancer Care, a national charity, to increase awareness of Asian women to services for breast screening, treatment, support and information and, as a volunteer, Kulsum provides one-to-one support to women with breast cancer having had that experience herself some years ago. She is the chairperson of the Breast Cancer Advisory Committee for a Health Authority, aiming to improve services to ensure high quality patient-centred care. As a council member of Breast Cancer Care she is working on improving access, especially for women of ethnic minority communities, by translations of literature and use of tapes. She also gives talks to medical students and Asian community groups on ethnic issues in relation to breast cancer.

Elected as a fellow to many medical bodies, such as the Royal College of Physicians of Edinburgh, the Faculty of Public Health Medicine and the Faculty of Pharmaceutical Medicine, Kulsum has become increasingly involved in activities to improve equality of access for minority groups since retirement.

# Tahira Amer Yousafzai

Tahira Amer Yousafzai

Tahira Amer Yousafzai was born into a land owning family in Pakistan in 1969. She studied in a Government high school in Attock City and a Government college for women in Rawalpindi. As the family were living in a rural area, there were no English medium schools, so after graduating from college, Tahira and her mother started a project in their area, which led to opening of an English medium school. Tahira played a key role in the success of the school with responsibility for advertising, recruiting, training, staff supervision and day to day management. Alongside the school which has been running successfully for the last 12 years, she also started a scheme for disabled children.

In 1988, Tahira married a British Asian and came to live in Britain. Having had personal experience and hardship as her first child, Mohammed was born with Down's Syndrome, she became aware of issues relating to disability and how it affects families. Initially starting her career as a Nursery Assistant in 1994, Tahira took up the post of residential social worker in 1995 because of her natural interest in the well being of the disabled and disadvantaged. Gaining experience, she then moved to Harrow Crossroads as the Asian Specialist Outreach Worker, where she assesses needs and provides assistance to physically and mentally frail elderly people as well as younger people with a disability. Since joining the organisation, she has achieved much success working for Asian carers, set up 2 support groups for Asian carers and made links with 250 Asian families with a disabled member.

In 1996, with sponsorship from Glaxo Wellcome and Kodak, Tahira organised a Diwali party for disabled and carers which was attended by the Deputy Mayor and 550 people.

Tahira's work at Harrow Crossroads was given an entry in the Carers National compilation The Black Carers Directory and she was invited to the launch of the directory at the House of Commons. She continues to campaign for the future of social care and has written to several MPs including Robert Hughes with whom she has met to discuss various issues, which have been raised by him during debates at the House of Commons.

As well as taking care of her own son Mohammed, Tahira fosters other children with Downs Syndrome. Her future plan is to co-ordinate with UNO and other organisation with the hope of being able to open a therapeutic centre in India and Pakistan for people with learning disabilities, as no such facilities currently exist.

# WOMEN OF SUBSTANCE
## Brief Profiles

*This book would not have been complete without also mentioning the following accomplished women, who have also contributed through their work.*

## Tanzeem Ahmed

*Confederation of Indian Organisations, 5 Westminster Bridge Road, London SE1 7XW.*
Tanzeem Ahmed was a Director until 1995, then a Research Officer and is currently a Co-ordinator at the Confederation of Indian Organisations, which exists to develop and promote the interests of the Asian communities in Britain through 6 main objectives. The strategy of the organisation is to develop its capacity to offer development support services which are culturally and socially sensitive, high in quality, readily accessible and value for money. It seeks to fulfil these aims through a specifically developed corporate strategy involving its values, the service expected and the resources available.

## Veena Bedi

*Hambrough Primary School, Southall, Middlesex.*
Veena Bedi is Head Teacher at Hambrough Primary School and participates in cultural activities as well as being involved on issues concerning women.

## Pratibha Gupta

*32 The Croft, Euxton, Chorley, Lancs PR7 6LH.*
A Senior Clinical Medical Officer in Family Planning, Dr Pratibha Gupta has been living in Britain since 1975 and is a happily married mother of 3 daughters.

# Jagjit Kaur Kohli

*30 Joseph Creighton Close, Ernsford Grange, Coventry CV3 2QE.*
Jagjit Kohli was born in Burma in 1940 and graduated with a First Class MA from Assam University. A keen sportswoman, she was a champion athelete for three consecutive years and, as a commissioned NCC Officer in India, she was accomplished in rifle shooting. As a teacher, she served in Anda Man Nikobai Islands before emigrating to Britain, where she trained as a Librarian and is an Associate of the Library Association. Jagjit is currently a Multi-Cultural Librarian in Warwickshire and organises library services to meet the needs of the Asian community, as well as co-ordinating cultural activities through schools, colleges and voluntary organisations.

Jagjit Kaur Kohli

Believing that everyone should have access to education, she raises funds for impoverished students through charity work. Profile 198

# Bina Mistry

*Zee TV, Northolt, Middlesex.*
Bina Mistry is currently Head of Programming at Zee TV and previously presented several weekly music programmes which introduced new releases and artists as well as the Asian Music Chart Top 10 songs.

# Shahnaz Pakravan

*BBC, White City, 201 Wood Lane, London W12 7TS.*
Shahnaz Pakravan is currently a Presenter on BBC's Tomorrow's World, in which capacity she travels extensively, researching for the programme. She also presented Women's Hour on Radio 4, which first went on air on Monday 7th October, 1946 and celebrated its 50th anniverary in 1996.

# Jassie Sahota

*53 Trinity Road, Luton, Beds LU3 2LN.*
Jassie Sahota is an accomplished Psycotherapist.

# Alpana Sen-Gupta

*102 Myrtle Road, Hounslow, Middx TW3 1QD*
An accomplished Kathak dancer and teacher, Alpana Sen-Gupta continues to give solo performances at local and national community theatres.

# Kamla Shori

*City of Coventry Housing & Environmental Services Directorate, Broadgate, Coventry CV1 1NH.*
Kamla Shori is a multilingual Senior Health Promotion Officer, managing Food Hygiene Training in six languages: English, Bengali, Hindi, Gujarati, Cantonese and Urdu. In this capacity, she has also developed teaching material in Food Hygiene in all six languages, including handbooks and videos in collaboration with Highfield Publications.

# Indu K. Shroff

*Flat 4, Friendship House, 67 Weymouth Street, Leicester LE4 6FP.*
Since retiring as Head teacher, Indu Shroff has taken up the post as Editor of two local magazines.

# Balmati Pooran Singh

*26 Benett Gardens, Norbury, London SW16 4QE.*
Balmati Pooran Singh is a retired State Registered Nurse and community worker.

# Mamta Yadav

*Top Floor, 24 Falkland Street, Glasgow G12 9PR.*
Mamta Yadav was born in India in 1958 and is a graduate in MA and Sangeet Prabhakar, which is equivalent to a BMus. in vocaldance and tabla. She is also an LLB and works as an Equal Opportunities Adviser for the South Lancashire Council Education Department. In her spare time, Mamta also works with the disabled and elderly within her local community.

*Names and addresses of the women contacted in the research for 'Women of Substance':*

Sudarshan Kaur ABROL M.B.E.
Mayfield School, Finch Road
Birmingham B19 1HP
Headteacher

Dr. Sushma D ACQUILLA
County Durham Health Authority
Appleton House
Lanchester Road
Durham DH1 5XZ
Consultant in Public
Health Medicine/ Lecturer
in Epidemiology & Public
Health Medicine

Bushra AHMED
The Legendary Joe Bloggs Inc. Co.
The Legendary Building
Bury New Road
Manchester M8 8FR
Marketing Director &
Music Artist Management

Samira AHMED
c/o BBC Newsgathering
RM 6234 Spur
TV Centre, Wood Lane
London W12 7RJ
Journalist

Tanzeem AHMED
Confederation of
Indian Organisations
5 Westminster Bridge Road
London SE1 7XW
Co-ordinator

Veeda AHMED
47 Ebury Mews
London SW1W 9NY
Artist

Anjana AHUJA
The Times Newspaper
1 Pennington Street
London E1 9XN
Journalist

Raj Kumari AHUJA
11 Brookland Road
Wigan WN1 2QG
General Practitioner
(Principal)

Najma AKHTAR
71 Berkeley Court
Baker Street
London NW1 5ND
Vocalist, Song Writer,
Composer

AMAR (Singh)
c/o Suki

Anita ANAND
ZEE TV
P.O. Box 139
Northolt, Middlesex UB5 5UT
Journalist-ZEE TV

Anupama ANAND
Norwood Gardens
Hayes, Middlesex UB4 9LU
T.V. Presenter/Artist

Indra ANAND
18 West End Avenue
Pinner, Middx
Director of Equities
MERRIL LYNCH EUROPE

Nasim ANWAR
54 Woodstock Road
Moseley
Birmingham B13 9BN
Manager Lansdowne
Health Centre

Leana ARAIN
30 Roland Way
London SW7 3RE
Barrister

Gursowinder ARK
9 Ladywell Court
Larbeet, Scotland
Pharmacist

Anu ARORA
University of Liverpool
Faculty of Law
Liverpool L69 3BX
Associate Dean Admissions
& Recruitment

Rani ATMA
74 The Avenue
London W13 8LB
Trainer-Counsellor (specialises
in marriage problems - director
and founder of Asian Family
Counselling Services)

Shamim AZAD
188 Perth Road
Illford, Essex IG2 6DZ
Writer, Teacher

Ramola BACHCHAN
RB Promotions Ltd.
195 Knightsbridge
London SW7 1RE
Self-employed
Runs a PR/Event
Management Co.

Kamlesh BAHL
Equal Opportunities Commission
Overseas House
Quay Street
Manchester M3 3HN
Solicitor
Chairwoman EOC

Rukhsana BAKHSH
14 Canterbury Avenue
Illford, Essex IG1 3NA
J.P., Head Primary Team
(Primary Coordinator)

Neelam BAKSHI
2 Broughton Road
Glasgow G23 5HW
Training & Management
Consultant

Anuradha BASU
Dept. of Economics
Univeristy of Reading
Whiteknights
Reading RG6 2AA
University Lecturer in
Management Studies

Shibani BASU
Mitcham Library
London Road, Mitcham
Surrey CR4 2YR
Community Librarian

Ramini BAXI
1 The Shrubberies
Chigwell, Essex IG7 5DU
Teacher, Inset Co-ordinator,
London Borough of Newham

Veena BEDI
Hambrough Primary School
Southall, Middx
Headteacher

Anita BHALLA
BBC Midlands Today
Room 195, BBC - Pebble Mill
Pebble Mill Road
Birmingham B5 7QQ

Zia BHALOO
Enterprise Chambers
9 Old Square, Lincoln's Inn
London WC2A 3SR
Barrister

Suman BHARGAVA
"SUMAN SADAN"
Herm Close, Osterley
Middx TW7 4RH

Usha BHATT
Sangam Association of Asian Women
Sangam Community Centre
210 Burnt Oak Broadway
Edgware
Middx HA8 0AP
President

Zarina BHIMJI
14 Downing Court
Grenville Street
London WC1N 1LX
Artist

Sudha BHUCHAR
Unit 19, Liddell Road
London NW6 2EW
TV Producer/Manager
Writer Asian Arts

Illa BHUVA
Community Worker

Malkiat BILKU
c/o Wally Kennedy
Support Campaign
Hillingdon Civic Centre
Uxbridge, Middlesex
Shop Steward

Chitraleka BOLAR
Chitraleka & Co.
Midlands Art Centre
Cannon Hill Park
Birmingham B12 9QH
Dancer and Choreographer

Gurdeep Kaur CHADHA
56 Sandringham Close
Haxby
York YO3 3GL
Cell culture Scientist

Gurinder CHADHA
UMBI Films Ltd.
15 Mornington Crescent
London NW1 7RG
Film Director

Tochi CHAGGAR
72 St. Pauls Close
Hounslow West
Middx TWB 3DF
Radio Broadcaster/
TV Producer/Director

Dr Qudsia CHANDRAN
Pantiles Medical Centre
Church Street, Sutton-in-Ashfield
Notts. NG17 1EX
General Practitioner

Debjani CHATTERJEE
11 Donnington Road
Sheffield S2 2RF
Writer, Storyteller,
Educationist

Anuradha Roma CHOUDHURY
2 Clos Yr Wenallt
Rhiwbina
Cardiff CF4 6TW
Librarian

Purba Rajlakshmee CHOUDHURY
London Arts Board
Elme House, 133 Long Acre
London WC2E 9AF
Press & Information Officer
London Arts Board

Maya CHOWDHRY
14 Sturton Road
Sheffield S4 7DF
Rashmi Choudhury
Freelance writer, Playwright
and Performance Poet

Jagjit CHUHAN
Fine Arts Dept.
Liverpool John Moores University
68 Hope Street
Liverpool L1 9EB
Artist (Painter)London
Part-Time Fine Art
Lecturer

Shama CONTRACTOR
116 Albert Road
Walthamstow
London E17 7PU
Administrative Officer/Teacher

Sarla COONER
7 Wylo Drive
Arkley, Barnet
Herts EN5 3JL
Orthodontist

Shirley Miriam DANIEL
7 Churchill Avenue
Kenton, Harrow
Middx HA3 0AX
OFSTED Inspector of Schools
Retired Headteacher

Mrs Jayaben DESAI
5 Brent Way
Monk's Park, Wembley
Middx HA9 6JN
Shop Steward

Indra Lavinia DEVA
169 Kennington Road
London SE11 6SF
Secretary to Nirj Deva (MP
until April 1997)

Hema DEVLUKIA
Ealing, Hammersmith & Hounslow
Health Authority
1 Armstrong Way, Southall
Middx UB2 4SA
Senior Manager & Community
Worker

Navdeep DHALIWAL
4 Morvin Avenue
Bhishopbriggs
Glasgow G64
Student (2nd year of BDS)
Shot Putt & Discus Thrower

Spinder DHALIWAL
CAER
Busines Studies Department
Southlands College
Roehampton Institute
London
CAER Director

Harjinder K. DHANJIL
ORIFLAME
Premier Executive

Jaya DHEER
105 Queen Margrate Drive
Kelvin Side
Glasgow G20 8PB
Director/Choreographer

Lucky DHILLON
Singer/Actress/Radio Presenter

Anuja DHIR
Chambers of J Matthew Q.C.
5 Paper Buildings, Temple
London EC4
Barrister

Maria FERNANDES
70A Teignmouth Road
Middle Temple
London NW2 4DX
(wife of Keith Vaz MP)
Solicitor and partner of
Fernandes Vaz Solicitors

Baroness Shreela FLATHER
HOUSE OF LORDS
Westminster
London SW1A 0PW
Member of House of Lords
Conservative Life Peer

Brij Lata GANDHI
10 Northampton Drive
Kelvinside
Glasgow G12 0AL
Community Worker

Sonia GANDHI
10 Northampton Drive
Kelvindale
Glasgow G12 0AL

Hema H GHADIALI
The Mount
North Avenue, Ashbourne
Derbyshire DE6 1EZ
Consultant Psychiatrist
Medical Practitioner

Chandra GHOSH
Broadmoor Hospital
Crowthorne
Berks, RG45 7EG
Consultant Psychiatrist

Sadhana GHOSE
431 Waterside
Chesham
Bucks HP5 1QE
Journalist/Lecturer

Zerbanoo GIFFORD
Herga House
London Road, Harrow on the Hill
Middx HA1 3JJ
Politician & Writer

Gurbans Kaur GILL
116 Bierton Road
Aylesbury
Bucks HP20 1EN
J.P., Stress Counsellor

Ms. Indpreet K. GOEL
7 Grantchester Close
Harrow
Middx HA1 3SW
Electronics Engineer

Ms. Sukhneel K. GOEL
7 Grantchester Close
Harrow
Middx HA1 3SW
Solicitor

Mrs Azmina GOVINDJI
"Littlecote"
Frithwood Avenue
Northwood, Middx
Freelance Dietician

Charanjit K. GROVER
119 Courtlands
Wolsey Road
Northwood
Middlesex
Justice of the Peace

Alpana Sen-Gupta
102 Myrtle Road
Hounslow
Middx TW3 1QD
Kathak Dancer/
Choreographer/Teacher

Indu GUPTA
"Vardaan"
1 Rassey Close, Limes Farm
Standish WM6 0BT
Medical Practitioner
Consultant Histopathologist

Pratibha GUPTA
MBBS 1974, DR.COG
32 The Croft
Euxton
Chorley, Lanc. PR7 6LH
Clinical Medical Officer

Rahila GUPTA
111 Chatsworth Road
London NW2 4BH
Writer

Nazim HAMID
Glasgow Council for Single Homeless
100 Picadilly Street
Glasgow G3 8DR
Administration & Finance Officer

Ayesha HASSAN
3 Dr Johnson's Buildings
Temple
London EC4Y 7BA
Barrister

Foqia HAYEE
212 Reigate Road
Bromley, Kent BR1 5JW
Schoolgovernor, Teacher
Mayor (Lewisham)

Roshan HORABIN
69 Seckford Street
Woodbridge, Suffolk
Retired Probation Officer
Counsellor/Lecturer

Shahrukh HUSAIN
29 Winchester Avenue
London NW6 7TT
Writer/Psychotherapist

Shehzad HUSAIN
10 Pickwick Way
Chislehurst, Kent BR7 6RZ
Cookery Consultant to M&S
Writer Indian Cookery
Restaurant Critic

Meena JAFAREY
Artsline
54 Shalton Street
London NW1 1HS

Sharmila JANDIAL
Glasgow University Man's Union
Hillhead
Glasgow G12, Scotland
President Glasgow Univ.
Man's Union

Annand JASANI
4 Upper Cliff Close
Penarth
Cardiff CF6 1BE
Broadcaster

Shobana JEYASINGH
Shobana Jeyasingh Dance Co.
The Place Theatre
17 Dukes Road
London WC1 9AB
Dance company founder

Dalia JOLLY
26 Vickery Court
40 Mitchell Street
London EC1V 3QL
Optometrist

Gunita JOLLY
26 Vickery Court
40 Mitchell Street
London EC1V 3QL
General Practitioner

Sujata JOLLY
8 Chestnut Close
Maidenhead
Berkshire SL6 8SY
Scientist

Mahmuda KABIR
2 Manor Park
Lee Green
London SE13 5RN
Team Manager Dept.
Social Services

Sandhya KAPITAN
The Wise Group
72 Charlotte Street
Glasgpw G1 5DW
Business Development
Manager

Ajeet Harbans KAUR
"Wazir Niwas"
10 Perryn Road, Acton
London W6 7LR
Justice of the Peace

Mrs Harbans KAUR
16 Belmont Avenue
Southall
Middx UB5 UHT
Retired Headteacher

Permindar KAUR
16 Hill Crest Grove
Sherwood
Nottingham NG5 1FT
Sculptor/Installation Artist/
Lecturer

Anita KAUSHIK
13C Woodland Road
Upper Norwood
London SE19 1NS
Artist

Nadya KASSAM
c/o Women's Press
34 Gt. Sutton Street
London EC1V 0DX
Writer/Editor

Mohini KENT
21 Thurlow Road
London NW3 5PP
Author, Journalist
Film Director

Lily KHAN
24 Marsh Avenue
Mitcham, Surrey CR4 2JN
Education-Homeless
Families Project-ILEA

Meher KHAN
16 Fencepiece Road
Barkingside, Essex IG6 2JX
Co-ordinator
Mayor 1994-1995

Qaisra Ehsan KHAN
16 Idmiston Road
London E15 1RG
Vice-Chair Newham
Education Committee

Sandra KHAN
Kingsbury Secondary School
Head of Year

Swinder KHANDPUR
2 Audley Road
Ealing, London W5 3ET

Razia KHATUN
22 Wilton Drive
Darlington, Co. Durham DL3 9PS
General Practitioner

Surendra KOCHAR
31 Monks Park
Wembley, Middx HA9 6JF
Actress

Kuldip KOHLI
15 Winton Drive
Kelvinside
Glasgow G12 0PZ
Community Worker

Jagit Kaur KOHLI
Librarian

Maninder KOHLI
Khubsoorat
6 Ealing Road, Wembley
Middx HA0 4TL
Designer/Businesswoman

Parveen KUMAR
St. Bartholomew's & The Royal
London School of Medicine & Dentistry
University of London
Digestive Research Centre
Charterhouse Square
London EC1M 6BQ
Consultant Physician, Reader
in Gastroenterology

Saroj LAL
13 Hatton Place
Edinburgh EH9 1UD
Primary School Teacher

Atiya LOCKWOOD
c/o Liberty
21 Tabard Street
London SE1 4LA
Press Co-ordinator

Grace Hermionie MACKIE
216 Mollison Way
Edgware, Middx HA8 5QY
Writer

Roshan McLENAHAN
4 Graftan Terrace
London NW2 6QC
Speech Therapist

Mita MADDEN
292 Essex Road
Islington N1 3AZ
Training Officer
(Social Services)

Shameem MAHMOOD
198 Canterbury Road
Leyton
London E10 6EH
Cardiac Rehabilitation Officer
Exercise Consultant, J.P.

Meenu MAINI
8 Woodrow Close
Perivale
Middx UB6 7HY
Civil Servant

Dr. Nageena MALIK
Flat 5
51 Besselsleigh Road
Wootton, Oxon OX13 6DW
Research Scientist

Bina MISTRY — Broadcaster/Musician
ZEE TV
PO Box 139
Northolt, Middx UB5 5UT

Rashida Shaikh A. MORBIWALLA — Self-employed Business
48 Prince Drive, Oadby — woman, community teacher
Higher Secretarial Studies
Leicester LE2 4SB

Syeda-Masooda MUKHTAR — Lecturer

Zenobia NADIRSHAW — Lead Clinician
Riverside Mental Health
Learning Disability Service
20 Kingsbridge Road
North Kensington
London W10 6PU

Kalpana NANDI — Consultant in Anaesthetic
322 Lordswood Road — Wolverhampton Hospital
Harborne
Birmingham B17 8AN

Surina NARULA — Charity Worker
Hyver Hall
Barnet Gate
Arkley, Barnet
Herts EN5 3JA

Aruna NATH — Senior Assessment Consultant
D.H.S.S. — Medicines Central Agency,
Market Towers — Dep. of Health
1 Nine Elms Lane, Vauxhall
London SW8

Geeta NAYAK — Principal General Practitioner
1 Calderfield Road
Liverpool L18 3HB

Deeyali NAYOR — Journalist

Lali NAYAR — Cookery Presenter/Writer
14 Sneyd Avenue — Programme organiser/
Westlands — Scriptwriter for ZEE TV
Newcastle-under-Lyme — Fundraiser
Staffordshire ST5 2PP

Jayantee NEBHRAJANI — Consultant Anaesthetist
106 the Ridgeway
London E4 6PU

Shahnaz PAKRAVAN — Television Presenter
BBC White City — BBC
201 Wood Lane
London W12 7TS

Pratibha PARMAR — Film Director
78 Fonthill Road
London N4 3HT

Sahera PASHA-GAMRE — Kathak Dancer
64 Gloucester Gardens
London W2 6BN

Bhadra PATEL — Librarian in Charge
30 Abbots Green
Croydon
Surrey CR0 5BH

Hansa PATEL — Advocate/Lecturer
16 Bengeworth Road
Harrow, Middlesex HA1 3SE

Indira PATEL — Community Worker
278 Coombe Lane
London SW20 0RW

Kanta Motilal PATEL — Community Development
104 Donaldson Road — Worker
Shooters Hill
London SE18 3JZ

Lata K.D. PATEL — Business Woman
67 Harrowdene Road — Councillor & Mayor of
Wembley, Middx HA0 2JQ — Borough of Brent

Vanita PATEL — Chair of Fundraising
Anti-Slavery International
Unit 4 Stableyard
Broomgroe Road
London SW9 9TL

Madhu Lata PATHAK — J.P., General Practitioner
84 Parkway
Gidea Park, Romford
Essex RM2 5PL

Lady Aruna PAUL — Patron & Fundraiser
Ambika Paul Foundation
Caparo House
103 Baker Street
London W1M 1FD

Usha Kumari PRASHAR — CBE, Director National
142 Buckingham Palace Road — Council for Voluntary
London SW1W 9TR

Kailash G. PURI — Writer, Advisor East West
6 Heaven Green Court — Family Advisory Circle,
Heaven Green — Public Speaking, Agony
Ealing W5 — Aunt, Yoga Teacher

Anjna RAHEJA — Managing Director
Media Moguls
Suite 34, Trinity House
Heather Park Drive
Wembley, Middx HAO 1SX

Sudesh RAHEJA — Ethnic Minority &
RAS Associates — Community Relations, J.P.
51 London Road
Stanmore, Middx HA7 4PA

Shama RAHMAN — Senior Lecturer & Course
The University of North London — Tutor, work placement co-
166-220 Holloway Road — ordin. & Dissertation superv.
London N7 8DB

Harsha RAI — Counsellor
124 Draycott Avenue
Kenton
Harrow, Middx.

Nina RAJARANI — Choreographer/Founder/
Srishti — Artistic Director
c/o Guy Chapman Associates
10-14 Macklin Street
Covent Garden
London WC2B 5NF

Sarita RAKHRA — Co-ordinator
The Asian Day Centre
Uxbridge College
off Coldharbour Lane
Hayes UB3 3DD

Veena Soni RALEIGH — Epidemiologist, Specialist
University of Surrey — in Health & Population
National Institute of Epidemiology
14 Frederick Sanger Road
The Surrey Research Park
Guildford, Surrey GU2 5YD

Ravinder RANDHAWA — Writer
59 Helix Road
Brixton
London SW2 2JR

Vasanthi Gangadhar RAO — Retired Headteacher
38 Ewell Road
Erdington
Birmingham B24 9EA

Mona RAPAL — Composer/Singer
71 St. Joseph's Drive
Southall
Middx UB1 1RP

Zaibby READING-SHAIKH — Director/Counsellor
EACH
Holdsworth House
65-73 Staines Road
Hounslow TW3 3HW

Ragini REDDY — Doctor-Gynacologist
5 The Green
Wylde Green Road
Sutton Coldsfiels B72 1JB

DJ RITU — D.J., Radio Presenter

Bharati ROY — Home-School Liaison
Top Floor Flat — Officer, Community
148 Freshfield Road — Education Tutor,

Brighton BN2 2HY — Community Interpretor

Sarita SABHARWAL — Promoter & Compere
S R Arts
26 Fermoy Road
Greenford
Middx UB6 9HX

Sultana K. SAEED — Lecturer (Law)
Apt. 68, 6 Hall Road
St. Johns Wood
London NW8 9PB

Jassie SAHOTA — Psycotherapist
53 Trinity Road
Luton
Beds LU3 2LN

Jaee SAMANT — Civil Servant
30 Regency Lodge
Adelaide Road
London NW3 5EE

Shaila SAMANT — Civil Servant / Executive Officer / Home Office
30 Regency Lodge
Adelaide Road
Swiss Cottage
London NW3 5EE

Daljit SANDHU — Senior Housing Manager in Special Needs Housing Assoc.
18 Derwent Road
London W5

Rita SANGHRAJKA — Learning Assistant
9 Tooke Close
Pinner
Middx HA5 4TJ

Zubedah B. SARWAR — J.P., Interpreter for Nottingham Health Authority
8 Middleton Boulevard
Wolloton Park
Nottingham NG8 1BH

Mrs.Yashveer SATHI — Company Director
58 Thorncliffe Road
Southall
Middx UB2 5RQ

Dolly SAXENA — J.P., Medical General Practitioner
93 Parkstone Avenue
Hornchurch
Essex RM11 3LP

Parminder SEKHON — Actress
c/o Hardial Rai
Watermans Arts Centre
Brentford
Middlesex

Robina SHAH — Psychologist, Independant Trainer & Consultant
15 Easton Drive
Cheadle
Cheshire SK8 2JD

Sharnjeet SHAN — Writer
c/o Amelia Fairney
Women's Press
34 Great Sutton Street
London EC1V 0DX

Anita SHARMA — General Practitioner
9 Norford Lane
Bamford, Rochdale

Nita SHARMA — Management & Training Consultant (own business)
Sharma Associates
47 Hessel Road
London W13 9ER

Seema SHARMA — Dentist
1 Deacons Terrace
Harecourt Road, Canonbury
London N1 2PH

Sabiha SHERIFF — News Editor
Sunrise Radio
Sunrise House
Sunrise Road
Southall

Kamla SHORI — Civil Servant
City of Coventry Housing and
Environmental Services Directorate
Broadgate, Coventry CV1 1NH

Indu K. SHROFF — Retired Teacher
M.A., B.T. Bombay Univ.
Flat 4, Friendship House
67 Weymouth Street
Leicester LE4 6FP

Hannana SIDDIQUI — Counsellor

Nahid SIDDIQUI — Kathak Dancer
c/o Sally Lycett
92 Windsor Road
Bexhill on Sea
East Sussex TN39 3PE

Surjit Kaur SIDHU — Psychiatric Staff Nurse (Retired)
19 Hambrough Road
Southall, Middx UB1 1HZ

Gurminder Kaur SIKAND — Artist Painter
63 Osbourne Grove
Sherwood, Nottingham NG5 2HE

Ajeet Harbans SINGH — Justice of the Peace
'Wazir Niwas'
10 Perryn Road
Acton, London W3 7LR

Amrit Kaur SINGH — Artist/Illustrator
27 Elleanor Road
Bidston, Wirral
Merseyside L43 7QN

Balmati POORAN SINGH — S.R.N. (Retired)
26 Benett Gardens
Norbury SW16 4QE

Kanwaljit Kaur SINGH — Education Inspector
43 Dorset Road
Merton Park
London SW19 3EZ

Rabindra Kaur SINGH — Artist/Illustrator
27 Elleanor Road
Bidston, Wirral
Merseyside L43 7QN

Rani SINGH — Artistic Director
Singh Theatre
91 Gunnesbury Avenue
Ealing
London W5 4LR

Sukhvinder Kaur STUBBS — Chief Executive Runnymede Trust

Asma Hatim SUTERWALLA — Co-ordinator UK Women's Conference / Interpreting & Translation Scheme in Mental Health
2 Georgian Way
Harrow-on-the-Hill
Middx HA1 3LF

Meera SYAL — Freelance Actress/Writer/ Comedienne
c/o Rochelle Stevens
2 Terretts Place, Islington
London N1 1QZ

Rekha TANDON — General Practitioner
Grove Health Centre
71 Grove Road
Wallasey, Wirral, LG5 3HT

Satinder Kaur TAUNQUE — Teacher
127 Petersfield Road
Hall Green
Birmingham B28 0BG

Damyanti THAKKER — Solicitor
Thakker & Co.
6 Churchill Court
58 Station Road
North Harrow, Middx HA2 7SA

Alka TRIVEDI — General Practitioner
West Leigh Medical Centre
West Leigh Lane
Leigh
Lancs WN7 5JE

Reshmi T. VARMA  
3 Woodcote Drive  
Purley  
Surrey CR2 3PD

Senior Consultant in Obstetrics
& Gynaecology

Merlyn Verona VAZ  
153 Scraptoft Lane  
Leicester LE5 2FF

Retired Teacher

Valerie Carol Marian VAZ  
65 Main Street  
Bushby, Leicester LE7 9PL

Solicitor

Veena VERMA  
47 Victoria Road  
Southall, Middx UB2 4EE

Social Worker

Jasbir VOHRA  
10 Brook Gardens  
Kingston, Surrey KT2 7ET

Tilusha VYAS  
35 Vardens Road  
Battersea  
London SW11 1RQ

Researcher/Journalist

Nina WADIA  
30 Shenley Road  
Heston  
Middx TW5 0AD

Comedienne

Sunita WALLIA  
34 Fourth Avenue  
Stepps  
Glasgow G33 6LB

Dietitian

Perween WARSI  
S & A Foods  
Sir Francis Ley Industrial Park  
37 Shaftesbury Street South  
Derby DE23 8YH

Managing Director

Kulwant Kaur WASU  
33 Lock Chase  
Blackheath  
London SW3 9HB

Multicultural Educ.
Advisory Teacher

Nelum P. WICKRAMASINGHE  
24 Llwynypia  
Lisvane  
Cardiff CF4 5SY

Part-time Teacher, Author

Amrit WILSON  
Flat 6  
34 Cross Street  
Islington N1

Writer, Lecturer

Kulsum WINSHIP  
1 Dudley Road  
Finchley  
London N3 2QR

Medical Prof.

Mamta YADAV  
24 Falkland Street  
Top Floor  
Glasgow G12 9PR  
Scotland

Equal Opportunities Adviser

Tahira YOUSAFZAI  
Harrow Crossroada  
62 Pinner Green  
Pinner  
Middx HA5 2AB

Outreach Worker

# OTHER TITLES BY HANSIB

## NAOROJI: The first Asian MP
A biography of Dadabhai Naoroji: Indian Patriot and British Liberal
**Omar Ralph**
Sailing through the history of time, there is a people whose forebears had ruled ancient Persia for five hundred years before the birth of Christ. A thousand years later they had become a refugee community who had fled to the west coast of India. Nearly a thousand years after that, one of their number rose to become the 'Grand Old Man of India' and the first non-European member of the British Parliament.
That man was Dadabhai Naoroji, and this book charts his story from a humble beginning in Bombay, to the time when he saw the foundations of modern India laid down. Unfortunately, he has not been remembered by many people, although he died within living memory, in 1917, and was a mentor to men such as Gandhi.
Published to coincide with the 50th Anniversary of India's Independence, this book hopes to re-live Naoroji's life story, so that the work he undertook both in India and in Britain can once again be understood. Illustrated with rare black and white photographs
**Paperback ISBN 976-8163-05-4 £11.95**

## BHOWNAGGREE: Member of Parliament 1895-1906
**John R Hinnells and Omar Ralph**
A biography of Sir Mancherjee Merwanjee Bhownaggree, Conservative MP for Bethnal Green, London, at the turn of the century. Much maligned in his day for allegedly forgetting his Indian heritage, his life and work as an MP in Britain and as an Indian statesman is now being re-assessed. This book was published to mark the parliamentary centenary of the first Asian Conservative MP.
**Paperback ISBN 1-870518-48-9 £3.00**

## INDIA: A Wealth of Diversity
This is as stunning and as compelling as its subject. Billions of words have been written about India, its many peoples and many languages, its diversity of cultures and religions. This book is a radical departure from the beaten track of previous books on India, bravely attempting in a single volume to illuminate with rare expertise, honesty and photographic and writing skills, practically every area of ancient and modern India. This does not pretend to be the definitive work on India, no work probably can, but it is certainly an appetite-whetter of high quality! Publication date August 1997
**Hardback ISBN 1-870518-61-6 £29.99**

## CORNERED TIGERS A history of Pakistan's Test cricket
**Adam Licudi**
The first ever authoritative history of Pakistani Test cricket, from its beginning in 1952 to the present, by Adam Licudi, former sports editor of the Asian Times, assisted by former Test star, Wasim Raja. With a unique collection of profiles from Abdul Hafeez Kardar, the first captain, to the giants of today, Wasim Akram, Waqar Younis and Inzamam-ul-Haq. This exciting and diligently researched book also honours Tigers like Hanif Mohammad, Fazal Mahmood, Imran Khan and Javed Miandad. Never before has there been so meticulous a chronicle of the highs and lows, the dramas and traumas of one of the greatest cricketing teams of all time with a sublime individual and collective talent. Here, too, is the Pakistani view of the 'sour-grapes' reaction and pettiness of other nations to Pakistan's spectacular rise to the pinnacles of World Test Cricket. Includes full scorecards from every Pakistan Test match and Test and One-Day averages for every Pakistan player.
**Paprback ISBN 1-870518-31-4 £16.95**

## PRIDE OF BLACK BRITISH WOMEN
**Deborah King**
A book which provides young people, particularly young black people who were born in Britain, with positive images and role models of women who they can relate to, identify with and aspire to emulate.
**Paperback ISBN 1-870518-34-9 £5.95**

## THE STATE OF BLACK BRITAIN: Volume Two
**Dr Aaron Haynes**
'The State of Black Britain: Volume Two', with a foreword by Peter Tucker, former chief executive of the Commission for Racial Equality, picks up where 'Volume One' leaves off and begins with an analysis of the Thatcher years (1979-1990) and their impact on the black experience. It updates the situation in employment, education and social services Law and order and the criminal justice system are put under the spotlight and there is an examination of black people and the media. Importantly, it ends with a black agenda for the start of the 21st Century. 'Volume Two' was launched on 18th May 1997 to coincide with the  London Borough of Haringey's Race Equality and Community Relations Awards, to mark the European Year Against Racism, 1997.
**Paperback ISBN 976-8163-04-8 £8.95**

## LEST WE FORGET
The Experiences of World War II Westindian Ex-Service Personnel
**Robert N Murray edited by Patrick L Hylton**
The participation of black soldiers in World War Two is a fact known by few people today. Even fewer are aware of the level of this participation, the number of men and women who served, the victories they earned and the many lives lost.
This book serves to enlighten people about the involvement of men and women from the Caribbean during the last war. It tells the story - largely through oral histories and personal experiences of the contribution made by them to that conflict and the subsequent settlement of a substantial number in the United Kingdom.
Illustrated with rare black and white photographs.
**Paperback ISBN 1-870518-52-7 £11.95**

## THE OTHER MIDDLE PASSAGE
Journal of a Voyage from Calcutta to Trinidad, 1858
**Introduced by Ron Ramdin**
Reproducing, in facsimile, the Journal of the Captain of the 'Salsette', a ship carrying Indian indentured labourers from India to the West Indies.
**Paperback ISBN 1-870518-28-4 £3.95**

## FACING THE CHALLENGE
A Report of the First National All-Party Convention of Black Asian and Ethnic Minority Councillors
Marking a key event in the history of British local politics. The  conference was attended by over half of all ethnic minority councillors in British Local Government and its findings are essential reading as Britain moves into a new millenium in which race equality will be high on the agenda. Published in conjunction with the Local Government Information Unit
**Paperback ISBN 1-870518-51-9 £6.95**

# A GUIDE TO VISITORS VISAS

**Maria Fernandes**

A step by step guide to anyone needing to apply for a visitors visa to the United Kingdom. It covers family, business, medical and transit visas, giving for each information on the documents required and and other factors that need to be taken into account when making an application. The guide includes and introduction by Home Secretary, Jack Straw.

**Paperback, Mapesbury Communications ISBN 1-899903-00-3 £3.95**

# A NEW SYSTEM OF SLAVERY

The Export of Indian Labour Overseas 1830-1920

**Hugh Tinker**

The first comprehensive historical survey of a hitherto neglected and only partially known migration- the export of Indians to supply the labour needed on colonial plantations worldwide, following the legal ending of slavery.

**Paperback ISBN 1-870518-18-7 £11.99**

# BENEVOLENT NEUTRALITY

Indian Government Policy and Labour Migration to British Guiana 1854-1884

**Dr Basdeo Mangru**

A detailed scholarly essay on Indian migration, which, for the first time, studies the Indian background of the indentured labourers.

**Hardback. ISBN 1-870518-10-1 £12.95**

*FORTHCOMING:*

# UGANDA: Africa's Secret Paradise

Commissioned by Yoweri K Museveni, President of the Republic of Uganda, this pioneering study and guide to the culture, environmental and scenic treasures, history and economy of one of Africa's most stable and secure nations. With a huge, relatively untapped industrial and investment potential, this book is indispensable for businesspersons, investors, diplomats and students of contemporary African history. With 320 full colour pages and a lucid text with a wealth of fascinating and practical information, this inspirational and informative work admirably captures the natural splendours of an ancient civilization, as well as its relentless and brave drive to modernization. Publication date September 1997

**Hardback ISBN 1-8700518-66-7 £25**

HANSIB

# TO ORDER ANY OF THESE TITLES

All titles available by mail order. Payments (by Cheque,PO or Visa/Access Credit Card payable to 'Readers Book Club'. Please add £1.50 p&p per book (UK), £3 p&p per book overseas. UK orders over £30 are post free.
To: Readers Book Club (Books Direct), PO Box 257, Welwyn, Herts AL6 9DH
Enquiries: Telephone 0171-281 1191 Fax 0171-263 9656